hand**made**
in Britain

handmade
in Britain

Appreciating Contemporary Artisans

Piyush Suri

Vivays Publishing
in association with
Handmade in Britain

Published by Vivays Publishing Ltd in association with Handmade in Britain

Copyright © text and design 2011, Piyush Suri

This book was produced by Vivays Publishing Ltd, London

A catalogue record for this book is available from the British Library

ISBN 978-1-908126-38-2

Publishing Director: Lee Ripley
Design: Tiziana Lardieri
Photography: Matthew Booth
Cover: Adrian McCurdy 'Cleft Oak Dish'
Printed in Slovenia

www.handmadeinbritain.co.uk   **www.vivays-publishing.com**

Preface

Handmade in Britain was set up in 2007 by Piyush Suri as an initiative to support and promote designer-makers who create their work in England, Wales, Scotland and Northern Ireland. The organisation aims to maintain high standards in the craft sector and to create market opportunities for buying and selling craft. One of the main goals of Handmade in Britain is to increase accessibility to the works of craftpeople by organising The Contemporary Craft and Design Fairs in Britain. These fairs also serve as a platform for up and coming designer-makers who are new to the business.

The first craft fair organised by Handmade in Britain was held in 2007 at Chelsea old Town Hall, London, where more than 75 talented British designer-makers from various disciplines including ceramics, fashion, jewellery, glass, metal, furniture, textiles and more, exhibited their collections to members of the public who were able to buy directly from the designer-maker or to commission new work. Over the past few years, Handmade in Britain has organised craft fairs in Bath and London and has also tried to promote British craft internationally by liaising with galleries in growing economies such as India and Turkey. In future, the organisation plans to collaborate with other organisations to arrange exhibitions overseas raising awareness about British crafts.
This book was created to support the resurgence of interest in high quality, handmade British designs and crafts. It features 90 contemporary British designer-makers who represent some of the talented artists working in Britain today.

Introduction

"Craft makes us feel rooted, give us a sense of belonging and connect us with our history. Our ancestors used t o create these crafts out of necessity and now we do them for fun, to make money and to express ourselves". Phyllis George

In an age when many people are more likely to throw something away rather than repair it, when some people want things yesterday instead of waiting until tomorrow, the idea of a product which is meticulously made by hand may seem like counterintuitive. In fact, there has been a real resurgence in the desire to own something that reflects careful craftsmanship; the more personal interaction between designer and material to create an end product with an attention to detail which you won't find in a mass-produced item. You not only own something unique, but you also know who created it.

Craft covers a wide range of areas from ceramics and glass to textiles and wood, from jewellery to furniture to fashion to pottery and more. It can be functional or decorative—or both. What all forms of craft have in common is that an individual has not only created a design but has also engaged with the materials and the process involved in making it. In other words, craft involves exploring the properties of materials as well as evolving processes and skills to produce beautiful, tactile objects which tell a story.

The designers included in this book, not only envision the product, but also generate it. These objects are not mass-produced, but personally crafted by the designer him or herself. The products they create are a result of their inspirations, influences and experiences. Each piece is handmade and reflects the interplay between designer and material to create a unique product of the highest quality. It is most appropriate, therefore, to call them designer-makers. And that is what this book is about.

Cultural Diversity

I still remember my first visit to London as a tourist when I was astonished to see its cultural diversity just by visiting different neighbourhoods and talking to a variety of people. I particularly fell in love with the craft and design scene, so much so that I decided to move to London and experience this big melting pot of culture. Britain has always been a diverse and heterogeneous nation and crafts have always been a strength of this country. It is the sense of free expression and individuality which is a huge source of inspiration for artists from any cultural background living here.

The designers I have chosen for this book represent the design and craft scene in Britain today. Coming from different cultural backgrounds and from as far away as China, Japan and the US, these designers have made Britain their home and continuously contribute towards the current resurgence of British crafts.

"The cultural diversity in Britain enhances the quirkiness and quality of craft and design".
Deryn Relph

Craft and Technology

Craft has always been associated with hand skills, but new technologies give rise to new opportunities. There is a different approach to craft these days which takes a more experimental view. The younger generation are making full use of technology, combining it with their hand skills to create and develop new materials, which fosters the fluid interaction among the disciplines. British design is constantly evolving as artists embrace changing technologies and continuously push the boundaries to come up with new solutions.

"The combination of tradition and craftsmanship with new technologies is very dynamic at the moment, new methods are being developed and people are revisiting traditional crafts with fresh eyes, producing great results". Sue Gregor

The Future is Bright

I have had the opportunity to work closely with designers and understand their work process. I see them revitalise the British craft sector through contemporary works that engage the attention of a new audience. This appreciation of handcrafted items is growing and it is refreshing to know that people are now ever more conscious of the origin of the products. Call me optimistic about the future of British crafts, but in this world of mass production I see a growing trend towards hand-crafted design as people are re-educated about sustainable and locally manufactured, handcrafted items. It is comforting to know that there are institutions like the Crafts Council and the many craft and design events running in the UK who support and promote the makers to develop their ideas and market themselves to a wider audience. Even the designer-makers view the future of craft and design with great optimism and believe their passion and the quality of their work will build a legacy, valued by others for years to come.

"Quality is the key, and I think that people are really beginning to understand the crafts movement. It is important that British design and crafts are supported and encouraged to flourish". Laura Marsden

"The amount of skilled work that has been created throughout Britain is breath-taking and the economic and social value of crafts and craftsmanship is becoming ever more popular. I think an increasing number of people value and celebrate British art and design". Ruth Emily Davey

"I do believe that in harder times, provenance and craftsmanship do have more meaning to consumers, so it's encouraging that quality of design and integrity of maker are all important factors still". Karen Dell'Armi

"British designers and artists have an edge and are not afraid to express themselves in an exciting unconventional way, so the future of British designs is in very safe hands". Chris Poupazis

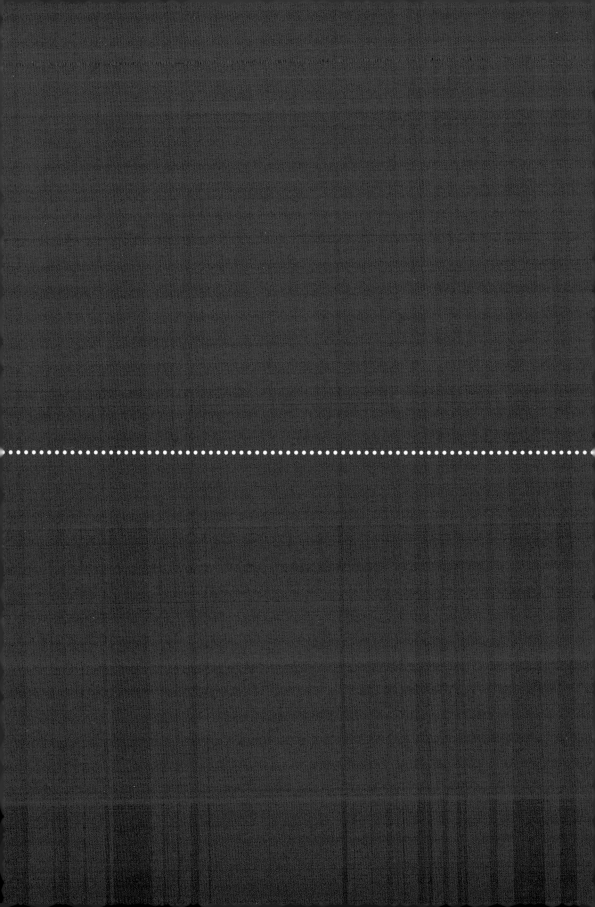

ceramics

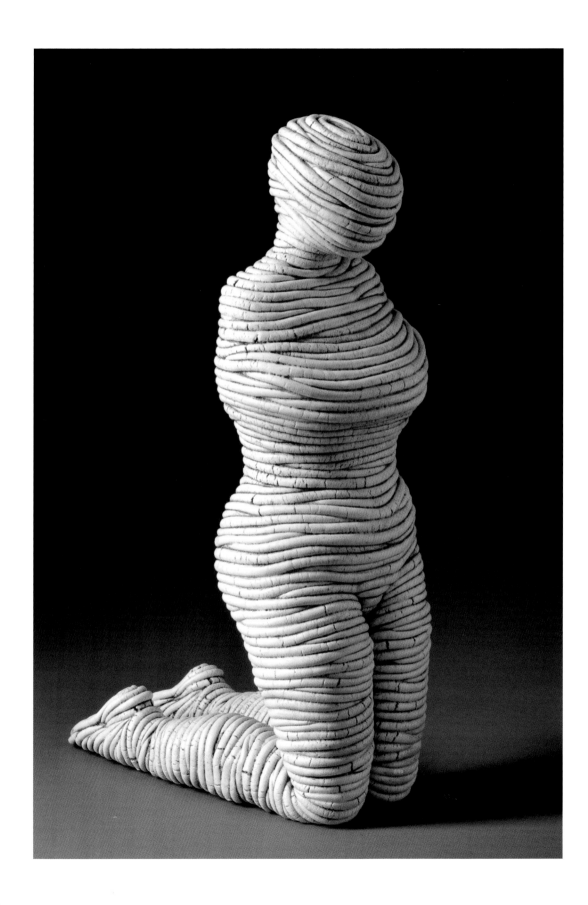

"Ceramics to me are a wealth of possibilities and realized emotions in clay. The art of ceramics never fails to lift my spirit".
Ferri Farahmandi

Kirsty Adams

www.kirstyadams.com   London

Connecting with clay in her own way

Since childhood, Kirsty has had a strong connection with clay and was always making things from clay, mud and other natural materials found in her garden. This connection has stayed with her ever since. She studied wood, ceramics, metal and plastics at the University of Brighton and then art and design at the University of Central England in Birmingham.

Natural elements, and in particular, seascapes stimulate her imagination and are reflected in her work. While studying in Japan, she was inspired by Oribe style of glazing which further developed her own methods of working.

She combines the influence of Japanese Oribe glazing with her own approach to throwing and glazing, using porcelain to produce pieces that are unusual and unique.

With a delicate style of throwing, pouring and dipping glazes, she creates a distinctive collection of thrown domestic porcelain ware. Each piece contains an element of spontaneity and refined throwing lines combined with the incidental marks of the glazing process.

Selected for the Nissin Noodle Bowl Grand Prix, Japan, she plans to run her own gallery and sell in international markets.

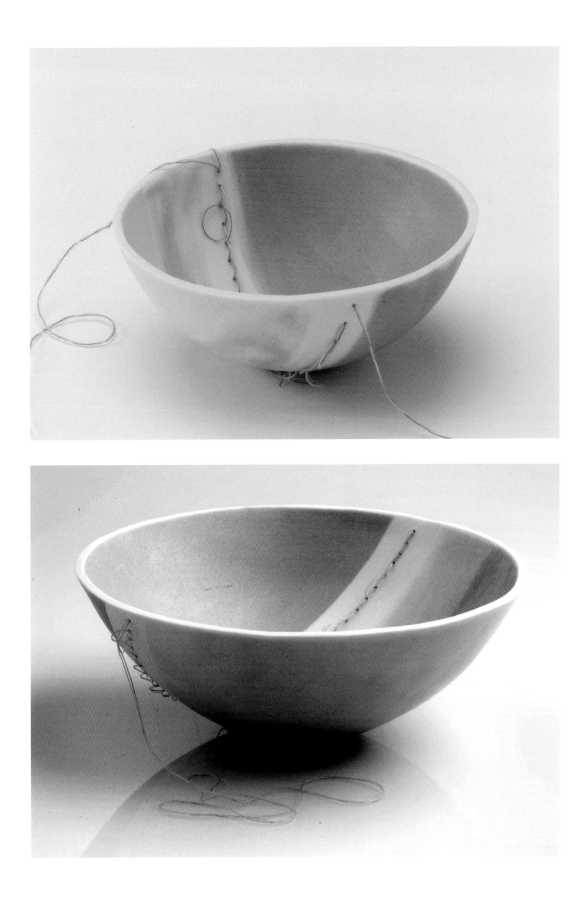

Cath Ball

www.stitchedceramics.com   Carlisle

Clay is her fabric

Encouraged by her art teachers at school, Cath continued with her art studies but hadn't considered it as a career. It wasn't until she finished her degree and went on to work in a pottery Cath realised she could make a living from it. She graduated from Cumbria Institute of Arts in 2004 with an applied arts degree and has been developing her skills in porcelain ever since. Working in the pottery alongside other designer-makers from different disciplines proved to be an excellent experience as it inspired her to start her own business.

At university she had also explored work on a sewing machine. The idea of combining the two disciplines — the hard surface of clay and the soft yarns used in textiles or embroidery threads — greatly appealed to her. Hence clay became her fabric, but textiles are her inspirations; whether it is texture, buttons, embroidery or hand stitching details.

Using a variety of techniques such as hand building, throwing and slip casting, her stitched ceramics collection challenges conventions through the development of an innovative technique.

Cath's future plans include opening a studio to support local and northwest ceramics artists in Cumbria.

Lucinda Brown

www.lucindabrowngallery.co.uk   Buckingham

Living the dream

Lucinda's passion for creating began early in life, encouraged by an artistic mother and grandmother, as there were no funds available for luxuries like toys in those days.

Later on, she discovered textiles, developing a flair for fashion clothing and eventually hats, and her collection of headwear was taken up by a major label in 1990. However, raising her son alone, trying to make ends meet meant that something had to give and the business suffered. This drew her into further education leading to her love for clay. Drawing faces and figures came as naturally to her as breathing, so translating this skill into 3D was both exciting and demanding as she learned to work with an unfamiliar medium.

Today she feels privileged to be earning a living from her art. She finds her inspiration from her connection with the Universe, the daily practice of meditation filling her with the serenity that becomes apparent in her sculptured faces.

"My purpose is simply creating beauty, to perfect my skills at the life-like interpretation of the human form and to leave the world even more beautiful than I found it". Lucinda Brown

Nicola Crocker

www.nicolacrocker.co.uk   Devon

The ceramicist chef

Originally trained as a chef and working in that field for ten years, Nicola's career took a back seat after she had children. She then enrolled herself in a ceramics program hoping to find a new direction. Now working full time from her home studio in North Devon, she identifies herself as a ceramicist and does not intend to go back to her previous career.

She draws her ideas from the coastline and rock pools where she lives. Every piece of her work is a progression from the previous one, which are sometimes the result of happy accidents. She uses stoneware crank clay or black clay for its sculptural qualities with a combination of slump moulding, pinching and throwing in her work.

Focussing on texture and surface pattern, she creates large sculptural vessels as well as small decorative pots for others to enjoy aesthetically. She enjoys the process of making as much as seeing how people respond to her work.

"I am interested in the nature of clay; the forms which I can produce from it, the colours and how the two can work together".
Nicola Crocker

Jo Davies

www.jo-davies.com   London

Lighthearted sensuality

Fortunate to have excellent facilities and support at her school's ceramics department, Jo used this opportunity to spend an intensive time creating ceramic art objects. It was only during her masters' studies at the Royal College of Art that she looked into the functional aspects of her work, providing a justification for being in the world.

Jo's work is about bringing together contrasts – wet and dry, wriggling and still, sharp and blunt. Each design is made of two contrasts, where the base might be solid, with more decorative, sometimes ambiguous counterparts. She uses decorative architectural forms to create objects that have a lighthearted sensuality, that move away from the formal rigidity of architecture, and into irregularity.

Jo tends to introduce humour by giving female names to her work highlighting an alignment with certain personality traits those names bring to mind. Combining the element of ridicule and sophistication, she creates an elegant style that sometimes teeters on the edge of vulgarity.

Her work is mainly about the exploration of clay and does not have a scripted narrative; it is instead the result of an intuitive enquiry into the material, using a visual language that gradually unfolds with each piece.

Janet Stahelin Edmondson

www.janetstahelin.co.uk   London

Exploring antique textures through porcelain

From a very young age Janet's creativity, heavily influenced by her family's history in the fashion and textile industry, was directed towards 3D design. As a child she spent hours making vessels from heavy clay soil in her garden dressed up in a beautiful silk dress given to her by her grandfather. So for her, beautiful fabrics and pots always went together. Her work today is the logical progression from those early childhood experiences.

Trained at Manchester School of Art (now Manchester Metropolitan University) in 3D design and specialising in ceramics and silversmithing, Janet works in porcelain, using lace, embroidery and crochet to add textural decoration on the hand built vessels she creates.

Using mainly antique Swiss lace from her grandfather's textile collection as a source of pattern, she unites textures, form and material in delicate but functional pieces with a very personal interpretation.

Her work explores the texture and translucency of fine porcelain.

Delfina Emmanuel

www.delfinaemmanuel.com   London

Expressing the precious life

Memories of Sardinia's coastline, rich in marine life, and festive memories of times with her family have been an integral part of Delfina's artistic approach to life.

After studying classics in Italy, she moved to London in 1974 to further her education and learn English. Over time, she had a family and England became her home. Unsure about what she really wanted to do, Delfina took several courses and ultimately found her passion in the form of clay, completing a degree course in ceramics at the University of Westminster in 2007.

Using a slow hand-building process, press moulding and slip casting methods, Delfina tries to capture the delicate and fragile nature of marine life such as corals, anemones and sea urchins in the hope of expressing the preciousness of life in her work.

She aims to make her objects visually attractive, but they go beyond use and have a symbolic meaning. In her teapots for example, she recognises the strong association with domesticity, tranquillity and the loss of individuality and the struggle in trying to regain it.

Ferri Farahmandi

www.ferriceramics.com   London

The human form

Raised in a typical Persian family in Iran, Ferri grew up in a very artistic and creative environment which shaped her experiences growing up. As a child, she explored different media such as painting, photography, and textiles to express herself but clay was always the material that excited her. Although art was never discouraged, the priority was to gain an academic education followed by marriage and family. This didn't leave any room for art in her life for many years. After moving to England and raising her children, she finally decided to pursue her dreams and enrolled in pottery classes. A degree course at Westminster University in ceramics followed.

Working mostly in stoneware and porcelain clay, Ferri's creations are hand-built and are heavily influenced by nature and organic forms. She continues to express herself through her work and to let her designs evolve and change organically like life itself. Fascinated by the human form, Ferri tries to show both physical and emotional aspects in her work in an attempt to give her pieces their own individual personalities. Her work explores issues of freedom and the restrictions of society in human lives.

Maria De Haan

www.noaceramics.com   London

Less is definitely more

Maria was inspired to train as a ceramicist at the age of 26 after extensive travel in East Asia. Essentially self-taught, her training began with evening classes followed by an apprenticeship at North Street potters in London. She also had one-on-one training by one of the renowned potters, Simon Leach, who taught her how to train her eye.

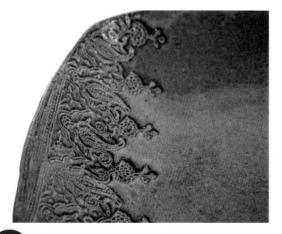

Looking for opportunities to learn more in her chosen career she moved to the tiny island of Bequia to work with another ceramist, Mike Goddard, in a 18th century sugar mill converted into a pottery studio. There she continued to learn and refine her work. She returned to London in 2008 to set up her own studio under the name of *Noa Ceramics* where she now works full time.

Maria makes functional tableware with Eastern influences, combining a minimal throwing style with traditional Indian designs. Her work is both wheel thrown and press molded and she uses antique hand-carved wooden printing blocks from India to decorate her work. Using a special white glaze over iron-rich clay, which adds definition to the print detail, her work has an almost vintage look. She uses stoneware clay for its strength and rustic charm.

She likes her ceramics to be tactile, beautiful and have a calming effect on people.

Shaun Hall

www.shaun-hall-raku.co.uk   Halstead, Essex

The raku specialist

Shaun's first contact with pottery was during a school trip to Colchester Castle in Essex, where he saw Roman artefacts and pottery vessels over a thousand years old. Later, he had a chance to handle some Anglo-Saxon pottery in his history class — an experience he never forgot! He studied art in college and specialised in ceramic design at Middlesex University. After graduation, a commission from Selfridges department store in London, attracted many clients. He currently lives in Halstead, Essex, where he also has his studio.

Shaun creates traditional wheel thrown glazed pottery and decorative hand constructed vessels. All his work is fired in a specially constructed raku kiln. Shaun's approach to raku differs from traditional Japanese raku and uses gas (and post firing reduction) instead of wood as a fuel. This method was pioneered by potters in the West. Involving a high degree of skill, it requires a physical interaction with the whole firing process and the results are often unpredictable.

One of the only potters to use a special copper matte raku slip (pioneered by John Wheeldon in the UK) Shaun's work has subtle reflections of nature coupled with architectural-sculptural form. The pieces are not strictly functional, but unique objects with a sense of mystery or ritual about them.

Zoë Hillyard

www.zoehillyard.com   Birmingham

Responding to cultural experiences

Zoë has always taken a constructional approach to creating fabrics, often inspired by traditional craft practices in Asia and Australia. In 2006, her interest in international craft development took her to Mongolia where she spent a year working at the Mongolian Textile Institute. Her experiences of the challenges of nomadic culture were an awe-inspiring lesson in design-for-survival. Inspired by the Mongolian

outlook on the ownership and significance of possessions and their resourcefulness in relation to materials, she has developed a new range of ceramic patchwork pieces which marks a rediscovery of her own creative language.

Using old silk fabrics to rebuild broken ceramics only with hand stitches to hold the piece together, Zoë creates completely unique decorative pieces. The variables include how vessels crack, the fabrics and thread choices, inside and outside construction as well as partial rebuilding, and provide infinite design possibilities in her work.

Working with materials that have already lived a life enables her to engage in up-cycling to create fresh reincarnations that leave mass produced anonymity behind.

For Zoë, design is all about problem solving, looking at issues from different perspectives to find fresh solutions within a contemporary context.

Andrew Hull

www.andrewhull.co.uk   Stoke-on-Trent

Humour is essential

As a child, Andrew fed the clumsy pelicans in the harbour at Paphos, Cyprus. Perhaps this experience laid the ground for what would be one of the biggest influences in his life as an artist: birds.

It was during his foundation course at Cambridge, that Andrew discovered the versatility of clay. His fascination with wildlife sculptures, however, began during his degree course at Loughborough College of Art & Design, when he did a project on the Martin Brothers (Victorian ceramic artists), which developed his skills for caricatured bird and animal sculptures.

Since then, he has spent the past 18 years as a sculptor and illustrator working for many studios in Britain developing fantasy ranges from animals in sporting themes, to mythological creatures like dragons, unicorns and Pegasus horses. In addition to birds and animals, he searches for different characters and personalities in people which serve as a great source of material. Still using the primitive method of carving into the clay, his individual pieces of work can take up to several weeks to create depending on the size.

His work has an audience reach from Australia to the US and South Africa and he promotes his work at international shows.

Hyo Soog Hwang

www.kelly-hyosooghwang.com　　London

Beauty of the rose

Hyo Soog grew up in a town in South Korea famous for its pottery. As a child she attended free lessons on the art of ceremonial tea making and it is while she was holding the tea bowl, that she noticed the beauty of the bowl in her hands. This experience prompted her to take short pottery courses and to pursue a degree in ceramic art. Since moving to London, she has since been studying a range of subjects from oil painting to art therapy to psychology and has done a masters degree at the Metropolitan University in London.

Hyo Soog Hwang, also known as Kelly, examines the influence of ceramic decoration in her work. She believes that application of ceramic decoration should consider both scientific and psychological aspects of decoration. These combine in her work to create rose-shaped pieces with colourful glazes which evoke an emotional response. This transformation of the rose's visual beauty into decorative art symbolises harmonised beauty which is expressed through the flower's delicate shape, colour and form. She works in porcelain, primarily on a potter's wheel, and with crystal glaze.

To investigate in depth the effects of colour and glaze on people's emotions, Hyo Soog is currently doing another master's degree in psychoanalytic studies at Goldsmiths, University of London to further inform her work.

Dameon Lynn

www.dameonlynnceramics.com   Cambridge

Elements of mystery

An inquisitive child, every time Dameon visited his late grandfather's antique shop, he wanted to know the stories behind the ever changing objects in the shop. This led on to his fascination for visiting museums and understanding the stories behind timeless ancient objects. After a family holiday to Italy, when he saw the magnificent architecture of the tower of Pisa, he was inspired to become a designer and this experience still informs some of his work.

His design manifesto is to create timeless ceramic objects that combine a strong form and presence with elements of mystery and exist somewhere between pottery and sculpture. Dameon currently makes his work using the potter's wheel. Due to the limitations of the wheel, he deconstructs and then reconstructs each piece to realise the form. The surface of the pot becomes a canvas capturing the momentum of the wheel and giving each form an additional element of individuality. He then paints the surface with layers of oxides and slips to add depth and colour to each piece.

Dameon has a deep interest in ancient Japanese philosophy where the idea of mind, spirit and soul connects man, material and process.

Lesley McShea

www.lesleymcshea.com   London

Punk potter who adores bats

With a fascination for bats and a huge collection dotted around the studio, well known potter Lesley takes her inspiration from most things – textures, natural forms, architecture and the world in general.

Brought up in Redcliff, Queensland Australia with its wide open spaces, dry textures and cliffs coloured red by iron oxide, she was surrounded by influences that she was able to bring to her future work. As a teenager she discovered ceramics through a Dutch classmate and has been passionate about them ever since.

She gained a thorough knowledge of glazing and firing techniques in Melbourne and although training in pottery would enable her to mass produce, she only ever throws a unique functional piece. Even when she makes pairs, each individual item has its own personality.

She creates stemmed ware, which involves combining components together; some wheel thrown, some heavily textured and press moulded. Her work ranges from very small items to architectural pieces.

Working towards a dream of having her own gallery space, Lesley continues to make one-off pieces and wheel thrown functional items.

Daniel Reynolds

www.reynoldsware.co.uk   London

Porcelain with a twist

When, at the age of seven, he saw his drawings being framed and displayed in the dedicated corner of the house by his father, Daniel identified art as a talent which he could develop further. Experimenting with pottery during classes at school, he found his love for clay and its endless possibilities as a creative medium. And it was while studying for a degree in furniture, that he combined his love for ceramics with making furniture and started to add porcelain feet and handles to the small wooden cabinets

he was making and creating stoneware table tops for his final year show.

Daniel mainly works in porcelain and stoneware, making hand-built vessels, translucent porcelain lamps and elements for mobile sculpture, based on natural forms, reminiscent of an 18th century tradition in English porcelain, but with a contemporary twist. He uses a slip cast technique and plaster moulds of natural and industrial forms to create unique items such as jackfruit and pumpkins, for example.

He also creates multimedia sculptures made of porcelain, copper, silver and glass as commission work for hotels and private collections. He exhibits regularly and his work is shown in many well-known galleries in the US and Europe.

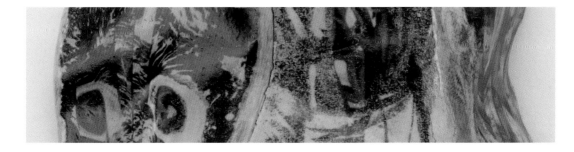

Denise Russell

www.creativeceramicsculpture.co.uk   Worcester

Nostalgia of a bygone era

Three years ago, while experimenting with combining textiles and ceramics as part of her master's degree, Denise realized that these disciplines could be amalgamated in perfect harmony enabling her to construct both installation and commercial pieces.

Inspired by the modern woman's distorted view of what constitutes the perfect female figure and influenced by her grandfather's depiction of everyday life in his own work back in the 60s and 70s, Denise uses her unique take on women's underwear, lingerie, and corsetry to depict the sensuous female form and the nostalgia of a bygone era. Combining porcelain with steel wool, fabric yarn and various metallic elements, she creates sculptures which are very unusual in appearance.

Denise plans to set up her own ceramic studio to promote contemporary ceramics and textiles to a wider audience within an innovative and stimulating environment. She sees a future where designer-makers produce a strong mingling of digital technology and traditional handmade skills to revolutionize the British design industry and insure its place in the future.

"I hope to keep British arts & crafts alive and kicking for future generations to enjoy".
Denise Russell

Kate Shuricht

www.kateschuricht.com   Kent

Telling stories through her work

Award-winner Kate's early love of ceramics came from her grandparents' collection of antique and contemporary pots from all over the world. Her first experience of working with clay was in her foundation course at university. She then specialised in ceramics and visual art at the University of Brighton. Since then, she has been making raku and slip-cast ceramics for exhibitions, commissions and collections.

Interested in conveying emotions and story telling through her work, she is inspired by his-

torical and contemporary boxes and the processes involved in creating them. Her trips to Japan in the 90s are still a source of inspiration for her work. Each process inspires a new approach and the unpredictable results in raku firing which she disliked during her studies, have now become her specialist area.

Conceived as small-scale installations, her elegant boxes, vessels and containers with their signature bound lids are sometimes combined with wood, slate or precious metal to create a sense of balance and harmony with the ceramics. Applying glaze onto her pieces like layers of fabric, Kate explores the qualities of surfaces with different finishes.

Her new series of curvaceous jugs positioned in intimate groups evoke a sense of movement and interplay, capturing fleeting moments of conversations.

Yueh Yin Taffs

www.yuehyintaffs.co.uk   London

I always liked big animals

Growing up in Taiwan's rugged countryside, Yueh Yin spent her childhood catching crabs and wild frogs with her brothers. She developed a passion for design and came to London to study fashion. Over this period she moved from fashion assistant in England to fashion correspondent in Taiwan, but she discovered her love for sculpture after visiting the British Museum. Yueh Yin was so inspired by Greek and Roman sculptures that she went back to university.

Yueh Yin loves big animals especially horses and they are favourite subjects in her work. Her horse sculptures merge all her experiences; the energy of the wild horses, the realism of the classical sculptures and the elements of styling. Instead of creating an exact replica she extracts the character, spirit and emotion of a horse and expresses it in her own unique way. She uses her imagination to capture the freedom of running wild and to make the emotions more 'readable' to humans.

In addition to horses, Yueh Yin likes sculpting bears making them lighthearted and funny.

"My pieces are art and are more than just a souvenir, they are something to keep".
Yueh Yin Taffs

Joy Trpkovic

www.joytrpkovic.co.uk   London

Porcelain is addictive

Award-winning Joy Trpkovic finds working with porcelain so addictive that she often works late into the night on her clay pieces, managing on only a few hours sleep most nights.

Joy's degree was in painting and it was not until her first job as a teacher that she discovered clay and the delights of experimenting with intuition rather than knowledge. She bought her first kiln and started working in hand built porcelain. She uses her hands and the simplest wood tools to pinch and carve her work. She relishes the risky nature of making fragile translucent porcelain pieces, testing the limits of the material and using the movement and shrinkage in firing to enhance the organic quality inherent in her work. Her use of colour as low fired lustre is an echo of her old water colour paintings. The land and sea based natural forms such as shells, rocks, or fossils serve as muses for her work.

Tracking heron's foot prints in the snow and counting 34 varieties of wild flowers in summer is what she recalls as her favourite childhood memories in Lancashire.

She has exhibited widely since 1979 in Britain, Europe and USA and her work is in private collections worldwide.

Shan Annabelle Valla

www.shanvalla.co.uk   London

Bringing new life to old curiosities

As a child surrounded by artists, art was Shan's favourite and strongest subject in school and it was natural for her to pursue this route into higher education. She then went on to do her masters from the Royal College of Art specialising in glass and ceramics.

Shan's designs are led by an understanding of the materials she works with, and the ideas evolve through the actual process of making. The key feature in her work is the quality of the materials, where she explores even accidental marks or imperfections and turns them into beautiful details with a mix of complex pattern and pure simplicity. Her work is a playful juxtaposition of pattern, surface, function and material, and the result is a delicate understated beauty, with a subtle twist on everyday life.

Mainly working in slip cast porcelain, blown and lamp-worked glass, she uses simple whites, greys, silver and gold. The other colours are introduced either in the form of flowers that the product holds or the interiors they sit in.
"Beautiful objects give me an overwhelming feeling of pleasure, and I have always wanted to create beautiful things".
Shan AnnabelleValla

Emily-Kriste Wilcox

www.emily-kriste.co.uk   Birmingham

Sense of repair and juxtaposition

One day Emily came across a chipped damaged old jug in a charity shop, which she noticed had been repaired numerous times. The pattern of these imperfections sparked her explorations into the sense of repair and juxtaposition which is the basis of her work.

After taking her first course in ceramics, working with clay seemed to come naturally

to Emily. She went on to study 3D design at Bath Spa University. The ability to respond to and converse with the three dimensional clay rather than working to a design is an integral part of the way she works.

The vessel form is the starting point and she likes to create a surface pattern in, around, and throughout the object exploring the space and composition much like a painting. Her work is hand built using predominantly a white earthenware body, and layers of surface decoration are built up in stages. In the process, the traditional tableware function is removed resulting in pieces which are playful, rich in movement, energy and aesthetic value.

Inspirations for her work come from a diversity of areas; dressmaking patterns, medieval puzzle jugs, maps, boats and landscapes. She is fascinated by work which has a sense of movement and energy as well as richly textured and patterned surfaces.

Norman Yap

www.normanyapceramics.com   London

Thrown stoneware and porcelain

Norman Yap, a self-trained potter who speaks several languages, was born in post-colonial Singapore but chose to become British. After receiving Susan Peterson's *The Craft and Art of Clay* from his partner, Norman changed his career from management consultant to full-time maker. He learned the craft by attending classes and also by observing, inquiring into, and being in the company of other professional potters. All of his hard work paid off when a buyer purchased his entire first collection and continues to ask for more to this day. Norman sits on the Council of London Potters.

Favouring the bowl, vase and bottle forms using either stoneware or porcelain, Norman goes for a minimal, clean design that allows the line to convey the personality of the piece. His pieces are thrown on a wheel and reduction fired (by restricting the oxygen supply) in a gas kiln creating richer celadon blues, greens and copper reds which are impossible to achieve with conventional electric kilns. His pieces have a curvaceous beauty and identity that are immediate.

His dream project? To create a framework of shelves rising from the ground to chest level in the form of a gown with a long train. His pieces would be positioned on each shelf with a naked Vivienne Westwood standing behind the creation, covered only in ceramics.

Glass

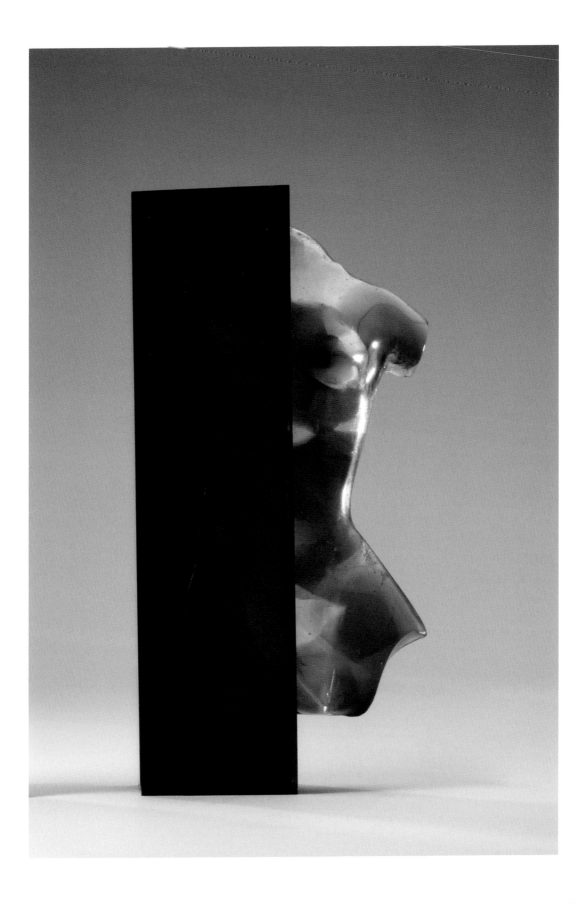

"Glass is one of the most exciting, colourful and pleasurable media for an artist to use. It can be transformed from the flat, sharp material to a tactile, glossy functional or aesthetic form. The result from glass casting provides an almost holographic image which is ever changing depending on the play of light". Isabel Mitchell

Adam Aaronson

www.adamaaronson.com   London

The abstract expressionist

At the age of four when Adam and his older sister bought their mother a small glass vase for her birthday, he had no idea that he would end up being a glass maker. It was a BBC documentary on Shoji Hamada that sparked his interest in ceramics when he was 16. Adam is a self-taught glass maker and a Fellow of the Society of Designer Craftsmen.

Living most of his life near rivers, lakes and sea, he never tires of looking at water which is a constant source of inspiration for his work. He is fascinated by the ceaseless mutability of light on the landscape, the sky and the horizons, which he depicts through his glass work.

He prefers to work spontaneously, beginning with an outline in his mind that evolves as he works. This evolutionary process builds and each piece leads to the next. A free blown glass vessel is manipulated into organic shapes and colour is used as an abstraction to create unique pieces that reflect his own perception of landscapes.

Jenefer Ham

www.jenefer.co.uk   Guildford

Flow and a sense of harmony

For Jenefer, opportunities to be creative as a child were never in short supply, whether it was hammering bits of wood in her father's workshop, making earthy bowls of garden mud, or painting.

Although she studied graphic design at university, she realised her preference was for creating tactile work. An opportunity to work for a jeweller came up and for a few years, Jenefer had an amazing time searching for gemstones and designing fine jewellery, before being lured back into graphic design.

Then, ten years ago, she was introduced to kiln formed glass and knew she'd found her calling. Since moving to England seven years ago, she's devoted herself to exploring glass making. Experimentation and cross-pollination from different media constantly provide new inspiration for her practice.

Her work is all about flow and a sense of harmony. Overlaying various shapes and colours, she creates new shades and shapes within each piece, building on her previous work creating beautiful and functional pieces.

Pieces from her best selling design, 'Tidal Pool', bring to mind sense of the relaxation, calm, and timelessness one feels while on a seaside holiday.

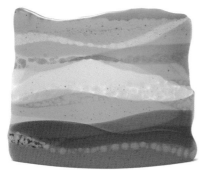

Caroline Lukehurst

www.carolinelukehurst.co.uk   Leamington Spa

Making beautiful objects of relevance

At the age of eight, Caroline won an elusive gold star certificate in her regional arts and crafts competition for her cake decoration and discovered that she loved making things for others to enjoy. The lesson learnt as a child was so relevant that it still shows in her work.

Since graduating in 3D design (craft) from Warwickshire College, School of Art, Caroline has been working from her studio in Royal Leamington Spa using both kiln fired glass

and precious metals. She creates kiln fired glass dishes and abstract molten glass wall panels with landscape images in soft shades of blue and grey, or warm shades of orange and amber depicting changing seasons.

Optimistic by nature she likes to make beautiful things which are relevant to the people today, work which reflects the pressures and pleasures of modern life. She draws her inspirations from the personal challenges faced by the individuals and by the positive approach visible within the beautiful environment around them.

Energised by Vivienne Westwood's uncompromising take on design, she loves the rebellious energy, enthusiasm and optimism which she aims to convey through her glass work.

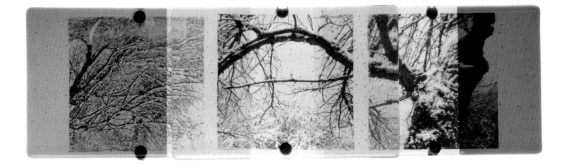

Isabel Mitchell

www.fusedform.com   Monmouth, South Wales

Science, art and sculpture

Since childhood, Isabel had her heart set on an art career but following careers advice from her school that "only dead artists make money" she took the science route and became a microbiologist. Even during her 25-year science career, she somehow continued with art as a hobby and attended clay workshops regularly. Five years ago, on receiving the gift of a week-long training course on glass making, she immediately fell in love with the material from the very first introduction and has continued to work in both clay and glass.

Her inspiration derives primarily from both her love for Italian classical sculptures and for the Abstract Expressionist artists who used colours so confidently. Her work focuses on the human form; the strong lines of the male form and the contours of the female form.

Her latest work on cast heads, influenced by the great Swedish glass artist Bertil Vallien, uses clay sculpted moulds or traditional 'lost wax' casting techniques to achieve depth and clarity. The result is an almost holographic image, ever changing depending on the colours used and the lighting.

Continuing her journey into glass casting, Isabel's work is all about trying new things which comes from her understanding of the science behind the technique and equipment.

Naomi Singer

www.naomisinger.co.uk   Cornwall

Petrol head country girl

From furniture built for dolls house to badly knitted tops for herself, Naomi always made things throughout her childhood. After an art and design foundation course at Weymouth College in Dorset, she studied contemporary crafts at the University College Falmouth where she started to work in glass and finally specialised in the material. Naomi combines both traditional and modern warm glass techniques, along with digitally manipulated images to create unique glass pieces.

Having spent most of her life surrounded by fields, trees and the sea, she uses flowers and seed heads found in and around her home in southwest England. She develops abstract patterns, which are fused between layers of coloured glass to create decorative wall panels, plates and bowls. Since moving to Cornwall, she sees its influence in the colours that have evolved in her work.

Even though her tableware is commercially successful, her heart lies in creating big statement wall panels, and sees her panels getting bigger and bigger in the future.

"Although my designs are very feminine and delicate using softer colours and floral images, in stark contrast I am a complete petrol head and love racing vintage minis on dirt tracks". Naomi Singer

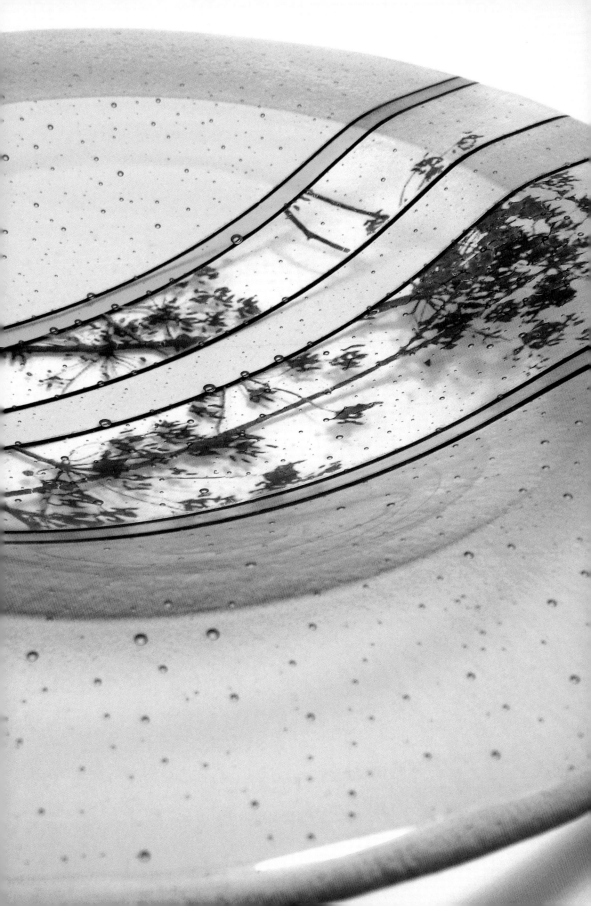

metal

"Metal is the most generous of materials to work with. It can be endlessly reworked, added to and subtracted from without losing its inherent qualities. It bends willingly to the creator's imagination". Nick Page

Chris Edwards

www.chrisedwards.eu   London

Reinterpreting and redefining everything

As a youngster, Chris Edwards spent much of his time taking apart and rebuilding whatever he could get his hands on, including wind-up gramophones, just to see how they worked. This need to know how everything works, encouraged by visits to the National Museum of Scotland where he was able to interact with the industrial models, resulted in model cantilever bridges, electric circuits, and even bangles from cutlery, plus the desire to reinterpret things and develop them further.

Memories, textures, materials, as well as the excitement of making something the world has never seen before drive Chris's manipulation of silver and gold to create innovative objects such as a dripping wax candlestick which defines the outline of an invisible bottle. His candlesticks, influenced by his interest in the surreal, are made using the 'lost wax' casting process to prepare the different components which are then assembled with traditional silversmithing techniques.

Chris also creates jewellery, combining traditional materials with pâté de verre (paste of glass) technique adding an exciting color palette to his work. The inspirations for the shapes come from pebbles as well as 60's and 70's design.

Having spent more than 30 years of his career as a production designer creating the "weird and wonderful" for films, television and commercials, he realized that silversmithing and jewellery were his natural calling.

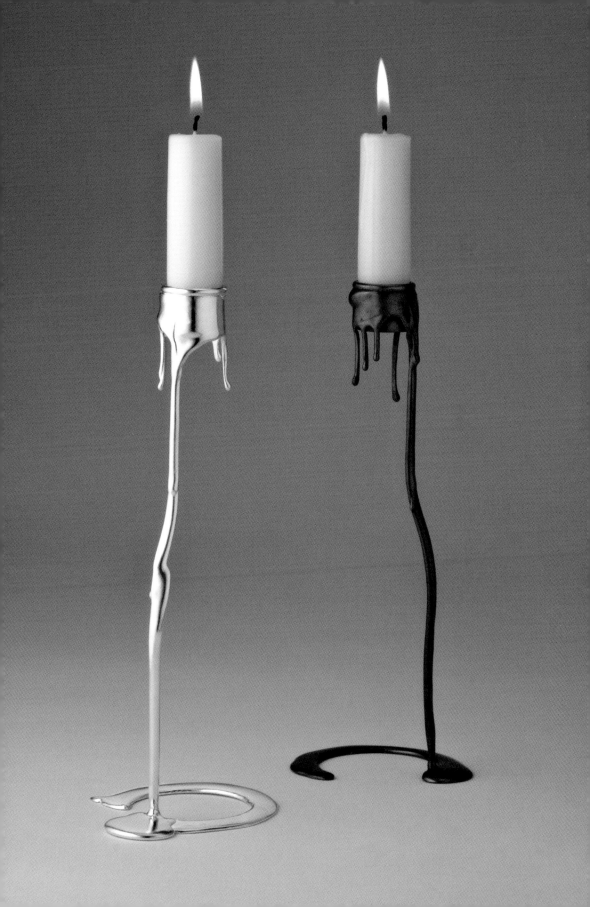

Philip Hearsey

www.philiphearsey.co.uk   Herefordshire

It's all about bronze

Wanting to be a painter since the age of 15, Philip spent a year in Camberwell School of Art before realising it wasn't his destiny. After leaving Camberwell, he spent the next few years working in the building and joinery industry learning some essential skills before focussing completely on design in 1975. He has devoted the greater part of the last ten years making vessel forms and table sculptures in bronze.

Using the architectural principles of simplic-

ity, elegance, honesty and timeless characteristics without unnecessary details, Philip uses a basic vocabulary of ovals, circles and triangles and their 3D counterparts to create elegant objects that possess an essential presence as well as intrinsic beauty.

Intrigued by the surface and the alchemy of patination, which presents challenging, unpredictable and seemingly endless possibilities, he thinks in bronze from the start to the finished object. Philip uses a sand casting process to explore and celebrate bronze as a material in its own right.

Enjoying the landscapes of the Welsh borders where he lives and works, he takes each day and its opportunities as they come.

"I love Sculptor Eduardo Chillida because his work embodies all the qualities to which I aspire". Philip Hearsey

Nick Page

www.fe26.co.uk   Manchester

Reorganising the environment around him

As a youngster creating dens and shelters in a grove of rhododendron bushes was Nick's favourite past time, it was this desire to modify and reorganise the environment around him that sparked his interest in design. With a degree in sculpture from Bath Academy of Art and a masters from Manchester Metropolitan University, he now works from his studio in Manchester.

His choice of using recycled materials is primarily aesthetic and is influenced by their inherent qualities. Interested in bare appearances rather than covered surfaces, he mainly uses natural materials like wood, copper and stone, but doesn't rule out man-made objects if they are in a state of decay from age and exposure.

His finished pieces are a collaboration between his instincts as a designer and what the material offers him as an inspiration to create one-off lamps and sculptures.

He has a growing desire to employ a low impact approach to making, which gives him the freedom to create while travelling.

Apart from his cat, he has never owned anything he hasn't modified or messed with in some way.

Janine Partington

www.janinepartington.co.uk   Bristol

Enjoying an unplanned journey

Growing up in a creative household full of her father's paintings and her mother's ceramics, Janine never planned to become a full-time designer-maker, she just realized one day that she had transformed into one! She had started creating while attending evening school to get a break from the stresses and responsibilities of motherhood. After selling her first pieces at small craft shows and local fairs, she was accepted by one gallery after another, until she truly became a professional designer-maker.

Following a design manifesto that asserts everything has a function, Janine taps into the natural world's wonders to form her unusual enamel designs. She creates her work by sifting enamel powder through hand-cut stencils onto bare copper. Her work is often described as "fresh, clean and contemporary" bringing tranquility to space.

Janine strives to strike the right balance between designing and making for money and simply for the love of the craft. She creates a series of scalpel-cut line drawings which explore the revealing and concealing nature of layering of line and form.

"Everything I achieve is a bonus as it was never part of any plan". Janine Partington

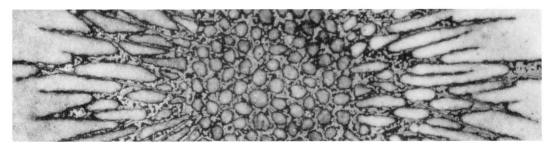

Eve Claire Taylor

www.eveclairetaylor.com   Hove, East Sussex

Tableware with a natural touch

At the age of 16, after attending evening classes in jewellery making, Eve decided this was the career she wanted to pursue. During college a full-time apprenticeship in the jewellery business provided her with experience in all aspects of design and in maintaining high standards while working under pressure.

Living in France for a while, she continued to work in jewellery before moving to Brighton, where she completed a degree in wood, metal, ceramics, and plastics at the University of Brighton as a mature student.

Eve specializes in highly tactile silver tableware, which is not only beautiful but also practical – perfect for special occasions and unique gifts. Rather than being traditional, her work contains an element of surprise, such as the unexpected detail found on the back of a leaf or inside a piece of bark.

Her work is a celebration of the entire natural phenomena that is taken for granted in the urban environment.

"I create my work in a very methodical meditative mindset to produce constructed beautiful and timeless pieces."
Eve Claire Taylor

furniture

"Our furniture should be an expression of ourselves and our personality through its shape, colour, texture and overall feel. It should be sustainable, functional and aesthetically enhance our surroundings, having a knock-on positive effect on our mood". Melanie Rye

Tim Chadsey

www.timchadsey.co.uk   Quarley, Hampshire

The essential beauty and elegance of wood

Born in Toronto, Tim came to England to study photography and worked as a still life photographer for 25 years. On discovering the beauty and quality of wood during one of his photographic assignments for a bespoke furniture company, he turned his creative focus to furniture making. Initially working on commissions for some of England's finest designers, he set up his own workshop in 2008.

His design sense, the essence of which is simplicity and elegance, is mainly influenced by the texture, colour and grain of the wood. Using British, European and North American hardwoods and (where appropriate) veneers, he draws on his understanding of light and shape as well as other inspirations such as architecture and nature.

In consultation with the clients' own ideas and imagination, he creates bespoke furniture handmade to the highest standards of craftsmanship, and the exchange of ideas with his clients often leads him to unexpected design solutions.

"Furniture made to truly good design rather than just following fashion is, and will always remain, of enduring appeal". Tim Chadsey

Tristan Harris

www.alternature.biz   Cornwall

Clean, simple and sustainable

Encouraged by his parents to earn pocket money, Tristan often found materials at home and made things to sell. It was this early hands-on approach that drove his ambition to manufacture. After his degree in sustainable 3D design at Falmouth College of Arts, Tristan started his company *Alternature* specialising in sustainable products and eco-design for the home.

Committed to clean design, sustainably sourced materials and excellent service, Tristan produces a range of products that are not only beautifully functional, but also have the least possible impact on the environment. Using local materials wherever possible, he even makes sure that waste is recycled; for example wood chippings are used by the local fish smoker and off-cuts of wood used to heat people's homes. Nothing is left to waste at *Alternature*.

Inspired by old furniture and traditional methods he doesn't get drawn in by trends and fashions, but still embraces the modern methods and styles in his pieces. With his work being sold as far away as Australia and Canada, he offers a range of products from elegant boot stands, frivolous cuckoo-less clocks, to custom contemporary furniture all hand-crafted in Cornwall.

Adrian McCurdy

www.cleftoak.co.uk   Jedburgh

Understanding the materials

Adrian grew up in a home that encouraged exploration of art, craft and music. Handling natural material was also part of his upbringing; Adrian used to help his father split oak logs. Unknown to him at the time, he had found the forte that defined him as a designer-maker later in his life.

He had studied painting and sculpture and then about 20 years ago, he was offered a commission by the Barley Hall, a museum in York, to replicate early oak furniture from around 1485. This opportunity to create period pieces in new wood, offered a way into both furniture and wood craft.

Inspired by scenic walks or simply rummaging through the wood pile, Adrian employs the little explored skill of using riven oak instead of sawn planks. This necessitates an adaptation of early craft skills to assemble the robust, curvaceous, and beautiful material to create his work.

With his work spreading as far east as South Korea and as far west as Hawaii, Adrian's real passion lies in creating contemporary designs using his personal design manifesto: *"understanding of the material, longevity in use and design."*

"I plan ahead not often more than six months, although my wood-stock might suggest differently". Adrian McCurdy

Melanie Porter

www. melanieporter.co.uk   London

Restoring the history to be the future

When Melanie happily played with her mother's yarns instead of her toys at the age of just eighteen months, her mother knew that she would be a maker when she grew up.

Destined to be a designer, Melanie completed a degree in fashion from Central Saint Martins followed by a masters in knitwear from Nottingham Trent University. Before deciding to turn her expertise to creating handsome,

up-cycled furniture, Melanie spent ten years working for a number of international fashion brands including Burberry.

Now, using the tools inherited from her grandfather, she combines traditional craft techniques with modern aesthetics and takes a very hands-on approach to her work. She sources chairs and other pieces from auctions and markets across the UK, which are then painstakingly stripped back to the frame, before being restored and reupholstered using traditional techniques. She covers those blank canvasses with a series of hand knitted, felted panels, especially created for each piece, using locally sourced wools and materials. The incredibly labour intensive process is done by hand, from the restoration and upholstery, to the felted, woollen panels and individual, crocheted buttons.

Melanie addresses each project individually, creating stunning pieces destined to became heirlooms.

Penny Price

www.pennypricefurniture.com   Somerset

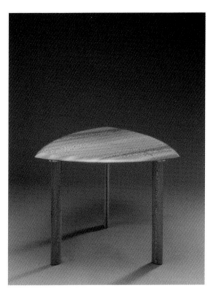

Less is more

Penny always showed a creative approach in her thinking, even as a child there were numerous occasions when her teacher and even her mother failed to understand her reasoning. Perhaps these were the first signs that she might become a designer. She studied furniture design and craftsmanship at Buckinghamshire Chilterns University College and set up her own company making high-quality finely crafted furniture.

Penny loves wood because of its versatility and tactile qualities and takes her influences from Art Nouveau, the Bauhaus and Art Deco. She likes to create pieces of furniture which could be viewed as works of art and yet retain the required functional aspects. She combines traditional craftsmanship and quality material with intelligent design, keeping it clean and simple.

Fond of one of the most influential architects of the 20th century Ludwig Mies van der Rohe, she shares the same philosophy of "less is more" in her work which is characterized by strict rules of measurement and proportion and precise attention to detail.

Penny is also a musician, songwriter and guitarist, and when she is not in her workshop making new furniture, she goes out and plays live at the local venues.

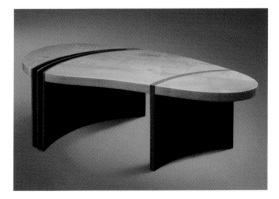

Melanie Rye

www.melmadethis.com   London

Post-modern vintage

Coming from a small village, craft played a very important role in Melanie's life and as a child she learned sewing, knitting, embroidery and many other creative skills from her mother. After graduating in textiles from Norwich, she moved to London where her initiatives in making her own furnishings led her to create her brand *Mel Made This*.

Inspiration drawn from anywhere and everywhere, Melanie loves pattern and colour spending her time in antique shops, boutiques, museums and galleries in search of something fresh and new.

Her impressive assortment of vintage patterned fabrics from the 50s, 60s and 70s are the starting point of her collection that includes upholstered screens, lamps, chairs and other home accessories. Once the fabric is finalized, she sources antique furniture and then the perfect trimming to give character to the finished piece. Using modern trimmings against traditional patterns and shapes in her work is "extraordinarily post-modern", capturing the essence of antiminimalist aesthetics.

Sustainability being central to her design ethos, she only works with natural fabrics and uses intricate hand stitching techniques to retain the intended texture of the fabric and trimmings and thus the furniture becomes a family investment with a story to tell.

textiles

"The fundamental nature of textiles to me is in the infinite diversity of colour and texture, the continual flexibility, creativity, and individual variety of design. The organic development of each piece as it progresses through the process of production to completion is constantly fascinating". Fleur Andreas

Fleur Andreas

www.fleurdesign.co.uk   Guildford

Exploring the possibilities

Originally a potter, Fleur studied textile design at a later stage in her career. When her youngest daughter went to university, Fleur enrolled at the University College, Farnham seeking renewed inspiration for her pottery and new artistic direction. This led to the challenge of studying for a degree in textiles.

Now working from her home studio, Fleur's work has evolved markedly through her use of natural materials. She has plans to create

a piece which involves all the processes from carding and spinning of the fleece, creating a yarn to dyeing, weaving and finishing.

Her work both as a potter and now as a weaver is inspired by the flow of the natural world and its changing seasons: in the infinite variety and subtlety of shades and textures as well as the effect of light and shadow. The greatest influence on her artistic life is her Uncle Anthony Pyke's incredibly detailed abstract paintings which seemed to capture the very essence of nature.

The tactile quality of ceramics and textiles plus their potential to fuse functionality with art continues to challenge and interest her resulting in the creation of unique, handcrafted woven pieces.

Michelle Appleton

www.michelleappleton.com   Manchester

Life is one big adventure

A member of Designers Eclectic based at Manchester's Craft and Design Centre, Michelle has always been fascinated with jewellery and objects that are handmade. To her every slight imperfection tells a tale and makes the object more interesting and unique.

Growing up, she always loved sketching and making things, her handmade birthday gifts for friends and family would be made up of all sorts of projects, most half finished or forgotten as she became distracted by something else. Artist, hair stylist, illustrator and now textile artist, Michelle finds that this area holds her interest and attention much longer than any other work she has done in the past.

Creating unique handmade woollen scarves, where no two pieces are the same, her latest work is influenced by research into Samburu (which means butterfly) tribal neckpieces. She aspires to create large textile-based pieces that appeal to the eye, as well as to the touch using different materials and techniques.

"British Design to me is a little bit like having a crush on someone, that feeling of excitement when you first come face to face with that handmade something which is new, special and unique. Lately I have had lots of crushes".
Michelle Appleton

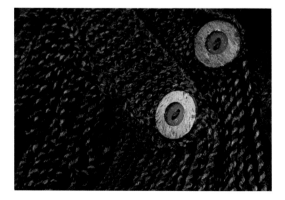

Helen Chatterton

www.perfectionofproduction.co.uk   Liverpool

It's all about fabric

Brought up in the northwest cotton town of Bury in Lancashire, in a textile obsessed household, Helen knew how to knit and sew at the age of seven, thanks to her mother who was a very keen and talented knitter and dress maker.

It wasn't until after the death of her parents, that Helen found the true extent of her mother's fabric collection which included vast quantities of fabrics and best of all an enormous quantity of Liberty Tana Lawn. She used those fabrics to create a collection of scarves and home accessories as a tribute both to her mother, who taught her everything about textiles, and her father, who taught her to love, care and respect items which have been well made. This collection has expanded into her award-winning *skinny scarves* and has been extremely successful.

Focussing on the use of colour in unusual juxtapositions, her work reflects different periods – mainly 1920s and 30s. She is passionate about all aspects of fabrics and yarns, experimenting with a wide variety of fabrics to create something beautiful that is immensely practical and hard wearing.

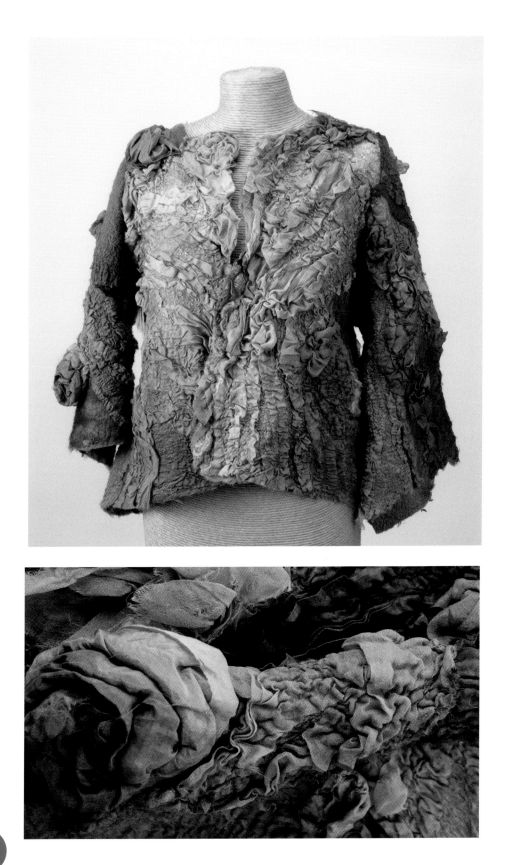

Chrissie Day

www.chrissieday.co.uk   Harwood, Teesdale

The fibre artist

Even at the age of four, Chrissie remembers holding needles and knitting alongside her grandmother, learning all about fibres. Knitting throughout her childhood, teenage years and most of her adulthood, she was then introduced to felting, and it was not long before she began her explorations with yarns and patterns.

Describing herself as a fibre artist, Chrissie loves experimenting by combining different fibres and techniques in an unusual way. She picks up her inspiration from nature, especially from the changing seasons and colours around her, and also from architecture that might catch her eye during her travels.

Her work sells widely and commissions keep her busy. She has started using new processes, techniques and fabrics together to create exhibition installations which will use digital enhancements as an alternative way of engaging with the process.

Chrissie is also a published author of six books on fibre art and spends her free time teaching others.

"My work is interlaced with soft memories and golden times of the past worked into every stitch, binding the piece together".
Chrissie Day

Zara Day

www.rosemary-rose.co.uk   Leamington Spa

Childhood memories of the seaside and gardens

Living in the West Midlands, Zara really misses the sight and smell of the sea which was the source of her strongest childhood memories. Her love for the remote beaches, beautiful shorelines and stunning views has informed her new collection of textiles and she draws on those memories to create her unique style. When not visiting the sea, her parents took her to botanical gardens; as a result traditional English roses and poppies have have had an impact on her design sensibility.

Zara creates beautiful textiles using hand felting, printing and embroidery techniques that are designed to reflect another time, creating a history of their own. Inspired by antique textile fragments found or inherited, her work explores feminine themes and trapped memories, revealed in layers like wallpaper peeling away to expose a lost past.

Using only natural fabrics, she uses her sewing machine as a drawing tool, creating spontaneous stitches, resulting in interesting surface decoration.

In fact for the last ten years, Zara has focussed solely on the use of stitch to draw and convey different qualities of line to illustrate a memory, story or capture an image. Her ever growing series of textile pictures has inspired a range of accessories and interior products.

Marie-Louise Denny

www.100-metres.co.uk   Cornwall

Eco-conscious knitter

After being encouraged in school to either work in an office or become a teacher, Marie Louise trained as a secretary. But her heart was always in designing and making clothes. When work experience in a fashion company gave her an insight into the design world, she decided to go back to school and study design. After sampling all possible art disciplines, she identified her passion for textiles and specialised in knitted textiles at Buckinghamshire College of

Brunel University.

Before moving to Cornwall and setting up her own label, London-based Louise designed for many design studios. In 2006 she launched her innovative range of luxurious hand-knitted accessories for fashion and home under the label *100 Metres*.

Her designs, inspired by organic pattern structure and textures, usually start with sketches and mood boards, which are then translated into knitting patterns. Using a rich colour palette and the finest quality yarns, she creates contemporary pieces which are comfortable to wear and sophisticated.

Committed to an eco-conscious and ethical approach to her work, Marie Louise also collaborates with other local makers in Cornwall who supply playful ceramic, metal and wood buttons that adorn her creations.

Wendy Edmonds

www.wendyedmondstextiles.co.uk   London

Create the unexpected

Having designed and made clothes for dolls throughout her childhood, textiles seemed to be the natural career path for Wendy. It was always one of the main things she was interested in.

She graduated from Chelsea College of Art and Design and then completed her masters from Winchester School of Art with a Crafts Council grant to set up her own studio.

She has a total obsession with the sun which not only makes her feel happy, but is also the theme behind most of her ideas. Inspired by the contrast of light and shadow on natural forms, she uses a heat transfer printing technique to create layers of textures with the resulting colours. Her work has an unusual tactile quality and is very stylish and practical.

She works on her own while printing and is not keen on anyone watching her or working in her space. Her philosophy is to get a buzz from working through her design process and achieving an end result she is happy with.

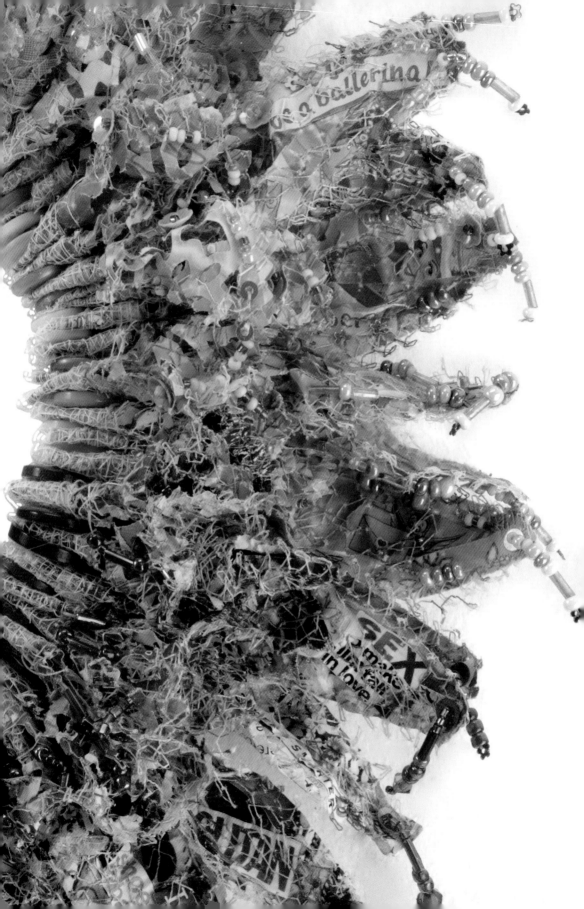

Jill Flower

www.jillflower.com   Westcott, Surrey

A late starter

After many years as an interior designer Jill decided to return to college in 2004 to explore and experiment with the techniques of stitched textile art, which she had always loved as a hobby. So what started as a hobby, became a full-time career and now she expresses her ideas as an experimental textile artist using different media, and both traditional and modern techniques.

A passion for colour, pattern and storytelling in her work comes from her childhood travels. She fondly recalls travelling from Liverpool to Lagos in a large ocean liner with her parents and being enthralled by the exotic locations and West African costumes and headresses made from brightly printed fabrics and this influence can be seen in her early work.

Her current work entails the use of paper which is deconstructed, reconstructed, stitched and washed exposing captions and print. Each piece is inspired by a speech from Shakespeare and the result is a stiff and lacy finish, reminiscent of an Elizabethan ruff.

"It is only very recently that I have become an artist able to express my own thoughts through textiles and fabrics". Jill Flower

Caren Garfen

www.carengarfen.com   London

Self-proclaimed perfectionist

Caren was born to be a designer-maker. Her mother, a seamstress, worked for a top fashion designer in the 70s, and her grandmother held exhibitions to showcase and sell the textile collages she made in her later years.

Caren, a self-proclaimed perfectionist, started off by using her skilled hands to sew miniature samplers for dolls' houses. She enjoyed great success in this field as her work was sold as far away as Japan and the United States. However, when it became time for a career change, she naturally switched to textile art.

Drawing inspiration from anything that might to act as a muse, Caren now uses her talent for hand stitching and silkscreen printing to address what matters to her the most: women's issues. She never goes into a project less than prepared, always exhaustively researching her topic before beginning the physical aspect of the work.

Even with such a serious issue and dedicated work ethic, Caren manages to balance the weighty with a touch of humour by stitching in motifs and text that lighten the mood. This mixture of the amusing with the somber has once again brought Caren Garfen international success as her work has been shown in The Netherlands, Hungary, the Ukraine, Wales, and Ireland with a concept store in Paris not far off.

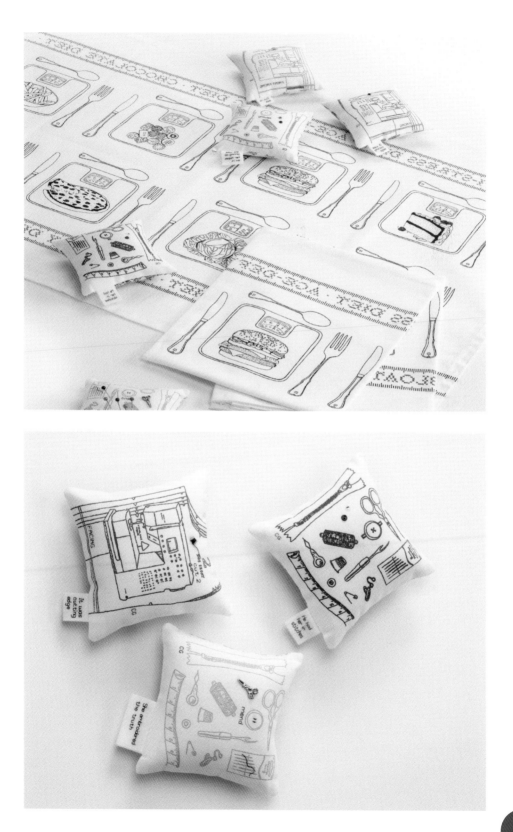

Kate Hasted

www.katehasted.co.uk   Tunbridge Wells

The world traveller

Nine years ago world-traveller Kathryn would never thought that her designs would be used as concepts and inspiration for fashion design collections by top designers in New York. it was then that she first bought all her printing equipment from a woman who helped her set up her studio and gave her a design agent contact in London.

Inspired by the 1998 "Structure and Surface" exhibition at MOMA in New York featuring contemporary Japanese textile designers, she uses old printing/surface techniques combined with modern technology.

Using hands-on processes such as Shibori, marbling, screen printing and hand dyeing, she creates strikingly innovative patterns experimenting with surface pattern and pushing the boundaries in printed textiles.

Having travelled around the world twice collecting ideas and experiences, the landscapes, people, different cultures, wildlife, architecture and her own memories serve to inform her work. She hopes to spend some time back in Australia visiting *Desart* the association of aboriginal art and craft centres to gain inspiration and learn about their artistic practices.

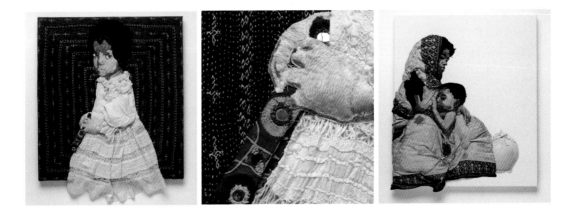

Aran Illingworth

www.aran-i.com   St. Neots, Cambs

Evoking an emotional response

With a love for antique fabrics, Aran searches auction catalogues and charity shops to find unusual fabrics for her work. Trained as a nurse, she only pursued design after her son started nursery school. With a first class degree in applied arts, Aran uses textiles as a medium to express her connection with undervalued women in Asian society.

She is inspired by Asia both for its colourful creativity as well as by its social problems. Motivated by her empathy with disadvantaged women and children, who become her subjects, her intention is to draw attention to the dire social conditions which persist in Asia.

Aran uses traditional embroidery techniques, appliqué and hand stitching to produce work that is modern and relevant to contemporary audiences. With a sense of form and colour inherited from her Indian background, she aims to evoke a clear emotional response through her work – whether that is compassion for the poor or milder emotions in relation to less politically charged subjects.

Although not a feminist, her work has a certain feminist sympathy which expresses her personal sense of connection with undervalued women in Asia.

Sara Keith

www.sarakeith.com   Stirlingshire, Scotland

Blending crafts and technology

Born into a creative home and growing up with a textile designer mother and an architect father, Sara remembers making things since an early age. Her family holidays on the island of Colonsay in Scotland awakened her appreciation of natural design and pattern making. She went on to do her degree in embroidered and woven textile design at Glasgow and then did a PhD at the University of Dundee.

Fascinated by the effects of time and the resulting patina on manmade and natural forms, she finds beauty in the imperfections. Following in the foot steps of admired Junichi Arai, Sara combines handcrafted skills with new technology to develop new materials. Using only natural fibres she creates tex-

tiles and jewellry employing a variety of techniques such as knitting, weaving, and crochet which are then treated with silver. Her fluid interaction between disciplines and playing, observing and listening to different materials results in unusual pairings and discovery.

Her fluid interaction between disciplines results in unusual pairings and discovery.

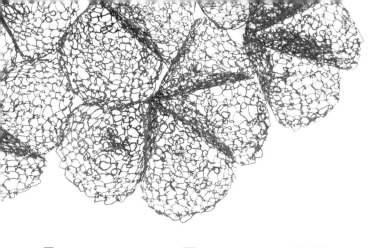

Laura Anne Marsden

www.lauramarsden.com   London

The eternal lace

Even at the age of five, Laura knew how to make a cushion from her vest. It was the satisfaction of having made an item herself which is the key designer-maker instinct. Following her masters from Chelsea College of Art and Design, she decided to develop her own techniques and took the challenging route of starting her own business.

With her lacework, she aims to preserve traditional techniques whilst using them in a contemporary and ecologically aware way. Taking inspiration from the past she gives new life to discarded plastic bags through her skills.

The lace is handmade using a yarn created entirely from waste plastic bags which is subjected to various processes resulting in a supple, stiff, water-resistant and delicate looking material. This eternal lace is then sculpted into wall adornments, jewellery and fashion pieces creating beautiful ethereal shadows reflected through its layers and are extremely light to wear.

Interested in historical garments, particularly Elizabethan lace cuffs and ruffs, it is the shape and stiffness of the lace portrayed in painting which inspire the shape of her work.

"I strive to challenge preconceptions about undesirable recycled products and demonstrate how waste can be reinvented".
 Laura Marsden

Carey Marvin

www.madeonce.co.uk   London

Let it fray

Carey grew up in a design-conscious and culturally rich family environment in New York in the 1950s. As a child, with plenty of unstructured time to herself, she constantly made things and by the very young age of six already saw herself as an artist. Several years later, following an artist's talk in her school, she tried all forms of art and those activities shaped her life and gave it meaning.

Before changing to the craft of stitching, Carey was a painter for many years and now uses the same skills in her embroidery work. Working everywhere, on buses and trains, in restaurants and theatres, even waiting in line, she rarely leaves the house without a piece of embroidery stuck in a pocket or hung around her neck.

Never planning and never worrying about mistakes, she just creates stitch after stitch until the end appears and there is no more to be done. From the start, the fabric off-cuts, vintage laces, broken threads, garments cut apart, are boiled and reformed to make the finished piece. Whether it is a framed wall piece, a dress or a shawl, each piece is unique and cannot be duplicated.

"Anything the needle can pass through can be embellished and through the process transformed and enhanced. Nothing is wasted".
Carey Marvin

Nick Ozanne

www.letoariadne.com   Gloucestershire

Everything Eric

From the National Gallery to glazed cakes and memories of school, Nick finds inspirations in a variety of sources and they are all personal interpretation of his experiences and his past. One of his favourite designs, for example, is 'Evelyn Waugh Stripe' where the colours echo moods from *Brideshead Revisited*.

He studied woven textiles at Winchester School of Art and the gift of a loom from his mother on his 30th birthday helped him to develop his style. Then in 2009, he launched his label *Leto & Ariadne*.

He uses only natural fibres such as silk and wool to create fabrics that are warm, tactile and luxuriously soft. His way of working is a direct reaction against the current throw-away culture where things are so readily available that they are no longer valued or cared for because they can be replaced too easily.

Nick cherishes the textiles archive room at the Victoria & Albert Museum which is filled with amazing fragments of textiles. He aspires to be as skilled as these unsung craftsmen and to create classic heirloom pieces which can be rediscovered and reinterpreted over many years.

By the way, Nick tends to name everything Eric, may it be his looms, plants or his bike.

Victoria Picon

www.loomtime.com   Nottingham

The Saori weaver

Having studied visual arts in Chile, Victoria moved to New York in 2009 where she was introduced to Saori philosophy and how to free her mind from aesthetic prejudices. She started practising Saori weaving under the guidance of her mentor Yukako Satone. Founded in Japan by Misao Jo in 1969, the aim of Saori weaving is to express oneself freely and pursue spiritual wealth through weaving. It involves developing a sense of self worth and willingness to live in the most satisfying way possible.

After moving back to Chile, Victoria explored the traditional Chilean textile culture through her loom and is now settled in England where she continues to create beautiful fabrics brought to life by Saori philosophy.

Sensitive to the natural life that surrounds her, Victoria's work is shaped by the origin and texture of different material that she finds. Her designs are inspired by the traditional form of origami, using minimal stitching to create a form that recognises the weight and natural movement of material and a philosophy of 'beauty with lack on intention'.

Her art project 'LoomTime' which is based in Nottingham is dedicated to spreading Saori spirit.

Donna Read

www.donnareadtextiles.com   London

Never rich but always content

Eclectic Donna, from a rural village of Oxford-shire, was the first member of her family to get a degree. With the support of her family she studied printed textiles at West Surrey College of Art and Design (now called University of Creative Arts, Farnham) and then pursued an advanced certificate in horticulture from the Royal Horticultural Society

She started painting by hand onto velvet using the material like a blank canvas, devising ways to fix and remove colours as she could not find the freedom or expressive quality for her work in any other medium. Since originating her craft on velvet, she has diversified, ex-perimenting with many different fabrics and now also works with silk, wool, and linen. Each fabric results in a work with its own individual look and feel.

Her ideas come from nature, whether it's a twig set against a blue sky, frou-frou cherry blossom or vivid orange lichen on a tree stump, she finds inspiration in almost everything. Vintage buttons and textiles, quirky 1930s prints and pottery or interior magazines also serve to fire her imagination.

Her work sells extensively in the USA and Japan. Her exclusive scarf collection for Pinto, Italy has been very popular in Europe.

Deryn Relph

www.derynrelph.co.uk   Portsmouth

Embracing the power of colour

Deryn's desire to create textiles came from never being able to find the right fabric for her school projects. Even at 15, experimenting with painted fabrics to make a pair of trousers was immensely satisfying.

After briefly studying science, she returned to education 20 years later to study what she had always loved. In 2010, Deryn graduated from Winchester School of Art with a degree in textiles, fashion and fibre, and received the Knitted Textiles Award from the UK Hand Knitting Association.

Deryn exploits the unique properties of knitted textiles to create an innovative range of interior textile products in a rainbow of colour combinations. Transforming natural structures, microscopic imagery and childhood memories into knitted textures and geometric patterns in bold colours, she combines her knitted pieces in a slightly mismatched way with purpose-dyed velvets and hand crocheted trims to produce a range of cushions, lampshades and furniture items.

With a retro feel to her work, Deryn hopes to bring a sense of happiness and promote a stronger bond between people and the things they own, so that her products can have a longer life. Using locally sourced natural yarns and up-cycling lampshades and furniture, she takes a sustainable approach to design with a minimal environmental impact.

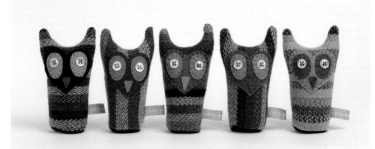

Sally Weatherhill

www.sallyweatherill.co.uk   Castle Hedingham

Half scientist, half artist

Growing up in a house full of modern classics, Sally always loved colour, whether in Scandinavian design products or colourful 60s designed curtains. Throughout her childhood and teenage years, she collected anything that came in sets of different colours such as squares of origami paper, tubes of smarties or jumbo packs of felt tips.

After obtaining a degree in art history from Brown University, Sally studied textiles at the California College of the Arts. She worked for several fabric companies before following advice from an architect friend to move to the UK because of its traditional textile culture. Her move, initially for six months, became permanent when she met her future husband.

Her work is influenced by techniques and experimentation, but is underpinned by her love and knowledge of modern art. Always with a camera by her side, she looks out for interesting patterns, textures and colours from the lid of a manhole cover, to an old church door, to the graffiti on the walls. When it comes to design, Sally trusts her instincts rather than following trends and keeps her designs simple. Considering herself half scientist and half artist, she experiments with different yarns and weaves, creating beautiful handwoven and jacquard fabrics.

fashion

"Just like a peacock extends its tail in a breathtaking display of colour, texture and pattern; fashion, for me, is the revelation of my creativity and desire to explore materials and surfaces. Fashion is my platform to express my vision and the body, a surface to display it". Natasha Wodzynski

Ruth Emily Davey

www.ruthemilydavey.co.uk   Aberystwyth, Wales

Making shoes to measure

Growing up in mid-Wales, Ruth spent her childhood in the Hafod, a late 18th century estate known for its picturesque views and breathtaking scenery. It was this pastoral surrounding that inspired creativity in both her and her siblings: All of whom went into different disciplines of art and design.

The process of becoming a shoe maker was a gradual aspiration. She spent three years in art college before a five year apprenticeship with Alan Raddon – shoe maker, designer and

reflexologist – led her to take up the profession.

Working from her workshop in mid-Wales, Ruth makes shoes to measure, also providing a mail order service for those who can't come to the workshop for a personal fitting. Working predominantly with very high quality full-grained Italian leather, she also incorporates a variety of fabrics such as checks and tweeds, heritage tartans, embroidered silks and brocades. Her handcrafted shoes are designed to last for years and can be repaired.

Once common on the high street, after the Industrial Revolution in the UK small-scale shoe makers have been replaced by large companies. Balvenie Young Master of Craft award winner Ruth continues to provide this special service by making shoes which are perfectly fitted to the shape of one's foot.

"The joy of handmade shoes is that no one else can wear yours". Ruth Emily Davey

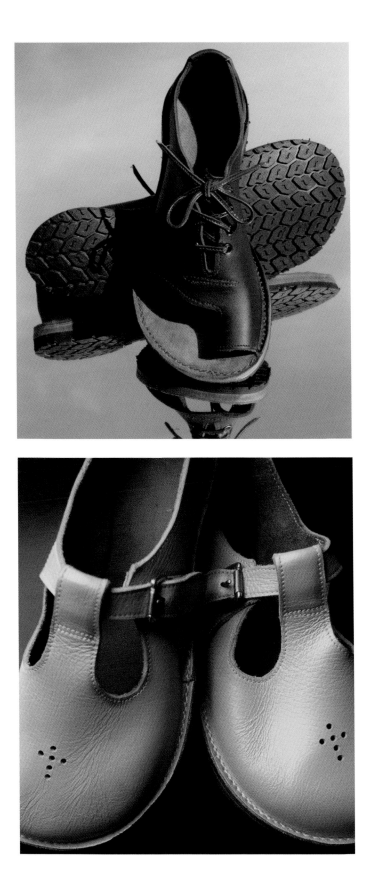

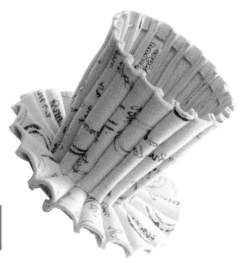

Gingerbread

www.gingerbreadhats.co.uk   London

Little bit of contradiction

Angela named her design label *Gingerbread* because she felt her work reflected the contradictory nature of its namesake, being both spicy and sweet.

Angela's love of headwear started with her own hair and as a child she experimented with bright hair, flamboyant extensions and accessories. While studying textiles at university, someone introduced her to millinery and she knew

immediately that this was what she wanted to do. She now considers herself an advocate of hats' accessible fun and expressive style.

Angela has a magic formula which she follows consisting of three things when designing and creating headwear – innovation in technique and design, quality of making and functionality.

Inspired by anything ranging from birds to postage stamps to rusted metal, Angela favours unusual, contrasting ideas and plays with shape and form combining traditional techniques with contemporary looks. For example, she likes to mix traditional millinery stock with unusual materials such as leather, plastics and metal chains to create couture pieces and occasion wear.

Amma Gyan

www.ammagyan.com　　Watford, Herts

Wear me, be you

Wear me, be you. This is exactly what Amma wants people to remember, to be themselves, discover who they are and keep things simple. And this is how she approaches her designs, making elegant and bold statements through strong use of colour.

It all began with making grass skirts at after school clubs and Barbie clothes on her miniature sewing machine, and much to her mother's disapproval, Amma decided to be a fashion designer at the age of nine. After her first degree in multimedia and information systems, she retrained as a pattern cutter and womenswear designer, allowing her to explore different media, eventually finding her love for leather.

Exploring the feel and diversity of leather, she combined her fashion and craft knowledge to launch a range of bags. But with the need to express her artistic desires, she mastered the art of moulding leather to create jewellery. Her latest work is constructed to illustrate freedom and movement, challenging the perception of how leather is used as a jewellery form and the concept of what is precious.

"When I work with naturally tanned leather, I'm reminded of the form that this once was and how grateful I am to create beautiful and challenging objects from it". Amma Gyan

154

Christianna Ibikunle

www.christiannaibikunle.com   London

Bespoke luxury for men

Her mother's obsession for handicrafts, from vibrantly coloured needle point cushions from America to knitting patterns from France, had such an influence on Christianna that she felt compelled to create her own things. Whether it was greeting cards for all occasions or birthday presents, the idea of being a maker was brewing in her for a long time.

With a post-graduate diploma in textiles from Goldsmiths College and a masters from the Royal College of Art in menswear accessories, Christianna uses all of her skills to create bespoke bags for the discerning urban male. Her bags are individually handmade using tra-ditional techniques and "cut edge" bag construction allowing the designs to be adjusted to suit the owner's requirements.

Drawing most of her inspiration from army bags, she combines high quality leather and felt with light-weight contemporary technical fabrics for the inside lining. Interested in new technologies, she enjoys manipulating materials and collaborating with other forward thinking artists.

"If I am going to add anything to the universe then it's got to be useful, beautiful and made to last forever and ever". Christianna Ibikunle

Yu-Ping Lin

www.yuxiart.com   Birmingham

The art of origami

As a child Yu-Ping Lin was inspired by her Aunt Lin Shu-Jen, a paper sculpture and mixed media artist in Taiwan, who showed her how to create artwork from everyday things. Thus Yu-Ping Lin painted on pebbles, branches or petals and explored new materials constantly.

After completing a degree in commercial design in Taiwan, she pursued her masters in jewellery and silversmithing at Birmingham City University and currently works from her studio in both fashion and jewellery.

Yu-Ping Lin is never without a sketchbook and constantly draws with different brush strokes as her ideas evolve and develop into more in-depth and detailed images. Her work is process based and structurally complex.

Appreciating the beauty in nature, her work focuses on the practices of origami and Chinese paper art, folding and pleating, architectural structures, organisms and forms inherent in nature and the interaction and seduction of pattern and colour.

Her experimentation with interaction also extends to food, mixing different materials in her cuisine, fruit with rice, and noodle with jam, for example. She enjoys trying new compositions in food and table settings which create an interesting game of experiencing colour and material for her.

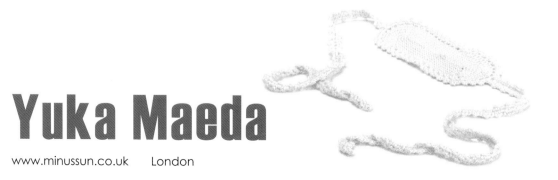

Yuka Maeda

www.minussun.co.uk   London

Creating her own world

Yuka does not like sunlight and never opens the curtains of her room. She wishes it was night all the time. Her world is sensual, dark, erotic and somehow naive with an atmosphere not usually associated with handicraft.

She makes things for the imagined girl of her dreams taking inspirations from her fantasy, films, music and books. The pieces are crafted with the greatest care and attention to the tiniest details reflecting the feelings she has for this ambiguous girl. Using natural fabrics within nostalgic silhouettes she creates fetish accessories for the girl she hasn't met yet.

She likes to create a world of her own and in order to keep her own work unique, she studies others who have their own worlds.

Her favourite piece is her embroidered bracelet which says "ARE YOU OKAY" on the outside as this is the question she fears the most and "I WILL BE FINE" on the inside as this response helps her to calm down.

Sally-Ann Provan

www.sallyannprovan.co.uk   Edinburgh

Elegance with a twist

Sally grew up in a house where everyone made what they needed, so whatever material was available, provided an ingredient to experiment with. Born in a family of joiners and cabinet makers, the urge to make has been in Sally's blood, but it wasn't until high school that she focussed on how to use her skills and become a maker.

With a degree in jewellery and silversmithing, Sally undertook both couture and theatrical millinery training in London and after working on several high profile projects she now creates bespoke modern millinery and accessories.

Influenced by mid-20th century design, particularly the 40s and the 70s, usually mixed with a dash of 18th century pomp or delicate Japanese flavour, her work is distinctive, quirky, elegant and above all wearable. She creates timeless feminine pieces using traditional techniques and a range of materials, which express luxurious elegance but with a hint of eccentricity.

Her favourite piece is her signature sculpted trilby made in over 30 different colours which sells all over the world.

"The wonderful things about hats and accessories are that they allow a woman to experiment with colour and express her personality".
Sally Ann Provan

Natasha Wodzynski

www.natwodproject.co.uk   London

Connecting nature and the man-made

When Natasha took offence at being advised to do a degree in textiles instead of fine arts, she chose to work in a bank and carried on painting in her spare time. Unhappy with her situation, she decided to move to London for a part-time course. She loved it so much that she left everything behind and came back to London to study at Central St. Martins College of Art and Design. It was only then she realised that textiles actually incorporated all the things she loved about being creative. Ironically, she ended up doing the degree in textiles at Chelsea College of Art and Design, which she had so strongly rejected in the past.

Natasha's textiles are heavily based upon experimentation with materials and techniques, triggered by her research. She takes her inspiration from the interaction between nature and man-made structures. The perfectly formed structures in nature, interacting with the man-made world bring beautiful juxtapositions of elegant and rough, deliberate and accidental results. This is what provides the visual material for her textiles. She is also fascinated by bio-technology and nano-technology.

"Design, for me, is about capturing a sensation, exploring materials and discovering new things". Natasha Wodzynski

jewellery

"Jewellery is that vital extra something that has endured from time immortal as a centrepiece for attention and a definition of who we are. It allows individual wearers within a culture, multiple opportunities to express themselves in truly personal ways. I love the way it can transform one's whole appearance, adding style and presence, giving the wearer a strong sense of stature and the feel good factor". Simone Micallef

Emma Baldwin

www.emmabaldwin.co.uk   Sheffield

Defying conventions

One summer Emma was introduced to finger weaving while spending a day at Warwick Castle. This early experience became the basis of what would become her later career making statement pieces of jewellery. Until the age of 18, however, she didn't realise that anything like the designer-maker occupation even existed. It was only after her foundation year that she investigated the options and pursued a degree at Sheffield Hallam University in metalwork and jewellery design.

Before becoming a jeweller, Emma was always interested in books, particularly fairytales, and thought of becoming an illustrator. She now uses illustration or an image as a starting point for creating something that has a story attached to it, something magical like a fairytale.

Ensuring sustainable and ecological practices in her design through recycling and responsible sourcing of materials, Emma tries to defy convention and use alternative materials along with precious metals whilst not compromising on design and quality.

Her reactions to most things in life are to use them as inspirations and to create pieces of jewellery that are more adventurous and truly special.

Gemma Clarke

www.gemmaclarkedesign.com   Suffolk

Exploring art in nature

Endless hours spent with her dad scouring beaches for tiny fragments of sea-glass and shells to make herself jewellery, finally paid off when Gemma found out that she could actually get paid for her creations as a jeweller. Her first introduction to jewellery was a work placement during school, which led her to study at the Sir John Cass University. She then had the opportunity to develop her skills by working for several well-known and established jewellers before creating her own collection. Gemma now designs and makes exclusive handmade jewellery from her studio situated in the Suffolk countryside.

Like many artists, she is inspired by organic forms and textures, exploring these art forms of nature in precious metals, pearls and vibrant semi-precious stones to capture and reveal the beauty of the natural world. She brings these elements together to produce work that is highly wearable, yet reflective of her own creative expression.

One of her works 'The Golden Acorn' creates an alluring modern day talisman. In English folklore, it is believed that if a woman wears an acorn tied around her neck, it will delay ageing due to the longevity of the oak.

Karen Dell'Armi

www.dellarmi.co.uk   Cardiff

Bold minimalism

After ten years in a successful marketing career, Karen decided to embark on a new journey in design where she followed her heart but used her head. She finished her silversmith and jewellery course in 2008 and has since won many awards, including the Welsh Women Mean Business 'Best Woman in Manufacturing Award' in 2011.

Karen takes a minimalist approach to design. Her work is a bold statement but is easy and light to wear. She is inspired by architecture, people, everyday emotions and objects as well as by the natural world. Her 'Serenity Collection' is inspired by Buddhist singing bowls, whereas her new collection 'Hope' is an interpretation of ancient lichens and mosses which she discovered on a charity climb to Mt. Kilimanjaro. She found the textures and patterns so interesting that she has recreated the random organic surface pattern by etching each hand-formed link to make large fluid chains then added rough, unpolished natural stones in vibrant colours.

She loves Ute Decker for her ethical sculptural jewellery and Marc Jacobs for his use of colour. Daily meditation helps her get through the demands of her growing business and she loves encouraging other young, talented designers to reach their potential.

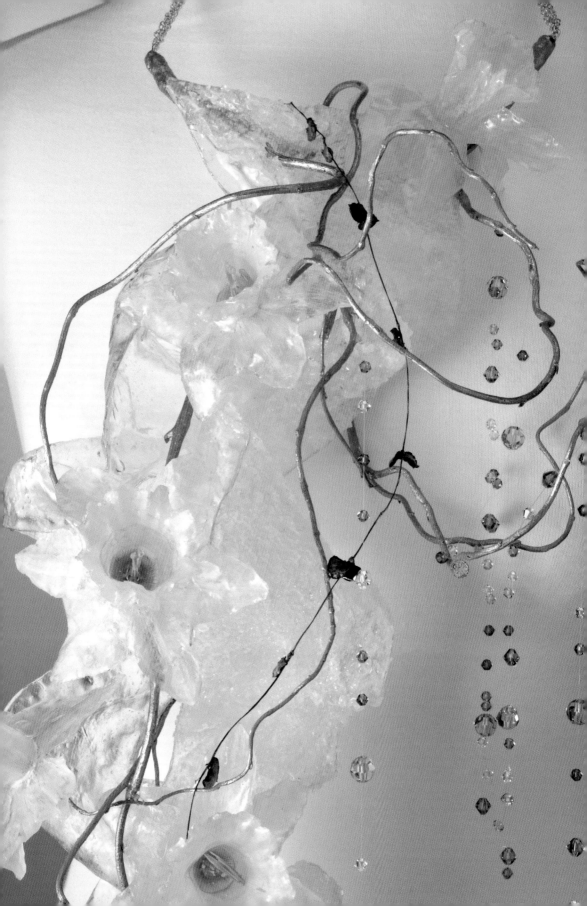

Fumi

www.wix.com/fumisgem/fumis-gem   Barnsley

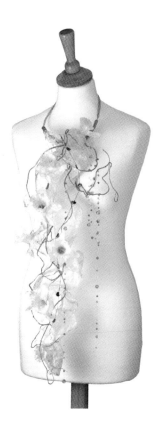

Extremely secretive

According to one of her former lecturers Fumi is extremely secretive and chooses to communicate solely through her work. Little is known about her life prior to moving to Britain about ten years ago. She avoids social situations preferring to spend long hours alone in her workshop where she creates her highly personal

sculptural objects and jewellery.

As a child, Fumi wanted to be a painter but during her early studies, her vision changed and she began to create wearable sculpture while on an Interdisciplinary art and design degree course at the University of Huddersfield.

She takes her inspiration from nature, which is the fundamental starting point of her work. Drawn to the transience and fragility of the natural world, she seeks to save precious memories that are captured in the form of special flowers. She preserves and strengthens the flowers by applying many layers of specialist resins and then combines them with other materials such as metals, plastics, fabric and crystals to give eternal life to someone's memories.

"People always told me I was eccentric, but I don't think so, I just do whatever I want to do at all times ". Fumi

Sue Gregor

www.suegregor.co.uk   Bristol

A marriage of nature and industry

The daughter of a prize-winning gardener, Sue has always been surrounded and inspired by plants. Finding the natural world spiritually uplifting, she captures the vitality of the plants in her jewellery.

She is intrigued by both the modernist approach to materials and the organic. Her work is a marriage of the natural and industrial worlds. Sue embraces new ideas and methods but believes old methods and new technologies can go hand in hand to create new work.

Using glass-quality acrylic, sterling silver, glass beads and silk threads, she combines both traditional methods and technologies such as hand dyeing, embossing, laser cutting and hand polishing to create unique surface patterns on her jewellery.

Alongside her best selling range of jewellery, Sue is currently developing a range of silk scarves with her organic patterns and has plans to design patterns for a building. She is looking forward to collaborating with the architects to create a building covered in plants.

She spends her free time in researching new innovations in art, design and technology which are a source of inspiration.

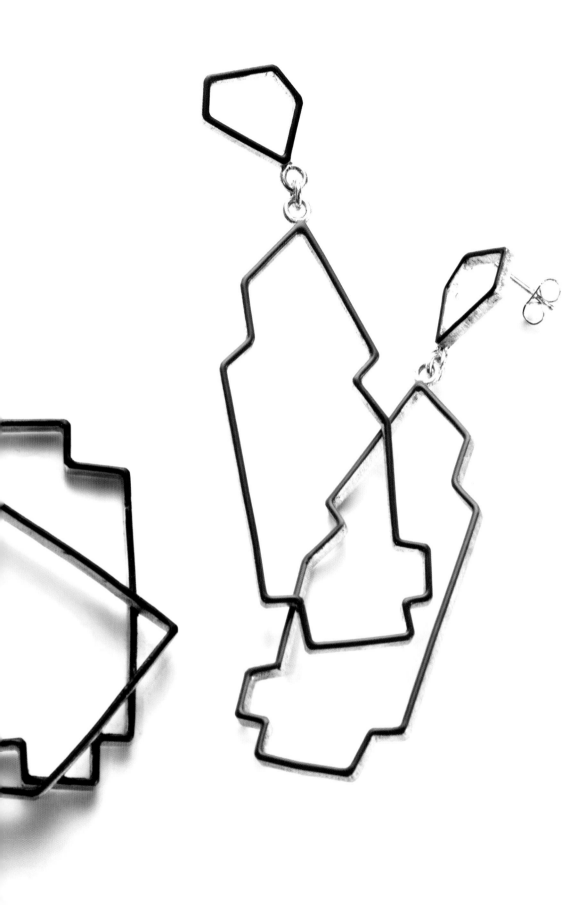

Marianna Hadass

www.mariannahadass.com   London

Shape and colour relationships

Marianna showed early promise as a designer when, at the age of eight, she made a collection of more than thirty pairs of miniature shoes from plasticine featuring different designs.

Born in the Soviet Union, she followed her passion for designing and making wearable items to pursue a masters degree in fashion and design at the Moscow State Textile Academy. Marianna then moved to the UK to continue studying the history of costume and completed her MPhil at De Montfort University, Leicester.

Jewellery making was always of deep interest to Marianna, who sees her move from fashion to jewellery design as part of her on-going development as a designer-maker. Marianna's jewellery consists of attention grabbing, colourful and funny statement pieces that are one-of-a kind or small collections of hand-made jewellery. Her work is inspired by.

The Russian avant garde, crafts and fairytales are all sources of inspiration, but her main interest lies in finding relationships between shapes and colours.

Marianna primarily uses silver as the framework and adds colour using semi-precious stones, enamel or Perspex.

"I believe that jewellery should express the wearer's feelings and emotions. Simultaneously, it should enhance and accentuate the wearer's most appealing features in a harmonious and understated manner". **Marianna Hadass**

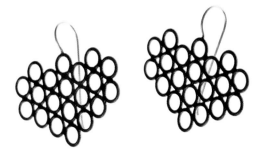

Zoe Harding

www.zoeharding.com   London

Going the extra mile to create luxury

Multiple award winner Zoe had never expected to be a jewellery designer until sixth form college when her sculptural jewellery experiments made with electronics wire and sheet metal from her mother's aluminium baking trays caught the eye of her tutors who encouraged her to continue. These experiments gave Zoe the confidence to explore further and learn jewellery making properly.

With a degree in metalwork and jewellery from Sheffield Hallam University, she took a diamond grading qualification and worked for Vivienne Westwood for four years. Now a member of the Institute of Professional Goldsmiths, Zoe runs her own label of fine jewellery as well as designing for other well known design houses.

Zoe loves hidden details and goes for a technically challenging aesthetic. Like a beautiful suit lining, she believes the inside of a piece should be as special as the outside. She likes unusual juxtapositions of shape, colour and materials which somehow work together. Best known for her triple-layered pierced bangles, where the inside shows an intricate pattern of a different but complimentary design, lined with beautiful natural materials such as glossy snakeskin or peacock feathers, Zoe loves creating luxury pieces.

Daphne Krinos

www.daphnekrinos.com   London

The urban influences

Despite her teacher's persuasion to follow an academic career rather than "waste her time on such a frivolous area", Daphne moved to London from Greece to study jewellery design. She was awarded a setting-up grant by the Crafts Council soon after she graduated and her work has been exhibited throughout the UK, Europe, US and Japan.

Her influences come both from Greece where she was born and from London where she has lived for the best part of her life. She loves cities, buildings, scaffolding, bridges, and all sorts of structures in various states of decay, as well as machinery and old tools.

She has also always been attracted to any coloured material that lets light through, like glass and precious stones.

Attracted to odd and unusual shapes, Daphne has a vast collection of translucent stones and her work is designed around them. Slowly evolving towards using gold, she usually works with dark oxidised silver which allows her to be spontaneous in her work.

Using traditional tools and techniques, she creates unique pieces which are not only elegant, but also timeless. Her more recent work is inspired by her love of old animation and street art.

Simone Micallef

www.simonemicallef.com   London

A love of bold colour

Although Simone left the sun drenched island of Malta, with its stone carved churches and beautiful dry stone walls and towering bastions, where she was born, its influences never left her. Simone moved to London to pursue a career in nursing.

Little did she realise quite how deeply her childhood impressions were embedded in her psyche and how much they were to inspire her later life. While working for the NHS as a midwife, she would relax and recharge her batteries by visiting art galleries and taking courses in art. She studied pottery, music, interior design and eventually jewellery in which she found her new identity. Her jewellery making still stems from a need to be creative, to make, to produce a beautiful end product just like a new created baby.

Her jewellery is born from stones dug from the earth in a glory of colours, then shaped and arranged with balance, colour and harmony. With her love of bold colour, the shapes of Matisse, Malta and her career as a midwife all influencing her work, Simone hopes her colourful necklaces will bring joy to women who wear them.

Anne Morgan

www.annemorgan.co.uk   Penarth, Wales

Organic textures and simple geometry

Having had a great passion for jewellery at an early age, Anne remembers as a child at Christmas when she could not wait for the crackers to be pulled so that she could adorn herself with treasures inside. That was when she knew that she would be a designer-maker when she grew up.

She graduated in 1996 with a degree in designed metalwork and jewellery and set up her first workshop in Cardiff. Anne is also a founding member and current chair of the Association of Contemporary Jewellery, Wales.

She mainly works with silver and explores the relationship between the look and the feel of the material. Her experimental techniques make her reticulated silver surfaces unique, these surfaces are offset with strong lines or colour from semi-precious stones. By balancing organic texture and simple geometry in her designs, the resulting pieces have a tactile sensuality.

Her recent collection is a combination of man-made and natural objects collected on the fantastic coastline of South Wales.

Eco-conscious and with a sustainable approach to her work, Anne uses non-conflicted semi-precious stones and diamonds and hopes to use fair trade gold in future.

Louise O'Neill

www.louiseoneill.com   London

Rhythms in the environment

Growing up in a creative environment, as both her parents were ceramicists, Louise always absorbed herself in the world of making things. Fascinated by the treasure trove of miniature ceramics, carvings, shells, seeds and curios collected by her mother which were kept in an old Japanese lacquered box, from the age of twelve Louise determined to become a jeweller; it seemed to fit her ideal, small scale and creative world.

After attending Reigate School of Art where there was a strong emphasis on drawing, she then completed her degree at Brighton. Working from her London studio, she identifies patterns in the natural and built environment around her and translates them into the flow and accent of her designs.

Louise works mainly in 18ct gold, often incorporating precious and semi-precious stones of unusual colours and shapes, notably aquamarines, sapphires, tourmalines or diamonds. She constructs folded and curved elements that complement the shapes and colours of the stones and sometimes highlights the edges of the metal elements to draw attention to a particular aspect of the piece.

Chris Poupazis

www.cjpoupazis.com   London

Relating to human experiences

Inspired by Robert Lee Morris's jewellery which Chris describes as 'poetry in motion' and Paulo Coelho's clear vision of the world and his understanding of human nature, Chris creates jewellery straight from his heart using precious metals and gems that relate to human experiences.

As a child, Chris loved spending nights watching the shooting stars with the sound of live music playing in the background after a hard day collecting shells on the beach in Greece. His father also played an important role in his future career by providing an apprenticeship as gold and silversmith in their family business.

His work is inspired by legends and myths, his photography, life's tiny structures, the Hackney marshes and anything that he feels passionate about. These influences can be seen in his work such as the lapis ring inspired from the ceiling of Canary Wharf Underground station and his 'Gaia' collection which is a tribute to Mother Earth.

"My designs know no boundaries, limitations or signature. I make individual pieces of art to admire, wear and have fun with".
Chris Poupazis

Caroline Reynolds

www.carolinereynolds.co.uk   East Sussex

Making jewellery, even in her dreams

Halfway through her window dressing course, Caroline decided she wanted to use her creative talents in a different way, so she followed the art route. A few years later, when she finished her degree at Central School of Art, she found her real niche as a jeweller. She gained experience working for other local jewellers, and then decided to start designing her own pieces.

Drawing inspiration from objects found in nature such as shells, seed pods and wood,

Caroline combines the simplicity of those shapes with their textured details to create handcrafted tactile jewellery. Working only with precious metals and quality gemstones, she uses highly skilled, traditional methods and prefers a matt finish on her work which adds a softness and depth to the pattern.

Her favourite design so far are her best selling, easy-to-wear 'Willow Rings', which are wrapped silver wires highlighted with 18ct gold granules.

Even making jewellery in her dreams, Caroline's goal is to make functional but beautiful jewellery, capturing the fragility of nature, and creating something that will have the timeless quality of an heirloom.

Alexandra Simpson

www.alexandrasimpson.com   London

Jewellery which caresses the senses

Alexandra grew up in London with a passion for travelling, discovering and experiencing new cultures. Not only a jeweller she is a singer, flute player and dancer. It was not until 2006 she realised that designing and creating jewellery would be her passion and life.

When designing, she starts by looking at the natural world; the way things move, the patterns of petals, the water's surface, reflections, shadows, forms....

Her inspiration, the way she designs and makes ensures she creates something enchantingly unique and different. Her jewellery has a delicate, romantic and graceful quality that caresses the senses.

With a playful approach to design, she hand carves her designs in wax, metal, glass or stone. She focuses mainly on quality, balance and composition to create exquisite pieces of jewellery which are special and can be passed down for generations.

Winner of Coutts New Jeweller award in 2009, Alexandra loves the fantasy and sensuality of Art Nouveau and knows something will be popular if she loves it.

Lesley Strickland

www.lesley-strickland.co.uk   London

The acetate specialist

As a child Lesley loved spending time with her grandfather in his wallpaper shop making things from wallpaper off-cuts. After leaving school, Lesley joined evening classes to study jewellery making at The City Literary Institute, London. Since then she has continued to evolve her personal style. Over the last thirty years Lesley has developed many new manufacturing techniques, either by modifying existing hand or industrial processes or by inventing new ones.

Lesley specialises in the use of cellulose acetate (derived from cotton oil) combined with sterling silver. She has developed special methods of forming, polishing and matting the acetate. Some pieces are decorated with silver piqué whilst others combine acetate forms with silver cast elements. Each piece is individually hand-crafted to a fine finish.

Inspired by weathered, natural forms and by sculptors of the 1950's, she designs pieces which are tactile and wearable. Not driven by fashion, she likes to create harmony in her work through colour.

Recognized internationally, Lesley's clients include the Museum of Modern Art in San Francisco and the Museum of Contemporary Arts in Chicago.

Lucy Jade Sylvester

www.lucysylvester.co.uk   Banbury,Oxfordshire

Preserving the wildlife

Growing up in the countryside making daisy chain necklaces and plaited grass rings, Lucy was always fascinated with the natural world. As a child, she collected feathers, twigs, shells, acorns, seeds, fallen birds' nests, dead beetles and flies, which she still keeps in a glass jar in her studio.

Her love for the British countryside has been the main focus in all her designs. Carefully making moulds from the forms she collects, Lucy fills the remaining cavity with molten silver and gold creating an exact replica of the original found object, preserved from the effects of time, to be worn and admired. The fine details of her jewellery are enhanced through colour and precious stones to highlight the delicate patterns and textures.

Since completing her masters in silversmithing and jewellery, she works from her Oxfordshire studio and has won many awards for her work. With climate change affecting wildlife, she wants her present work involving insects and plants, to become a record for the future.

"Each new season or place visited brings fresh inspiration and objects to work with".
Lucy Jade Sylvester

Catherine Thomas

www.ctsilver.co.uk   Wimborne, Dorset

Blending traditional and modern techniques

Growing up in a scientific environment, Catherine was fascinated to observe natural forms, whether the amazing patterns created by sunlight shining through the leaves or the complex nature of the fern. She was always encouraged to take notice of the environment around her and this now inspires most of her work.

Before stepping into the world of jewellery, Catherine studied languages and lived in Paris for five years. When she returned to the UK, her passion for craft and design was rekindled. She attended a number of short courses learning bench skills and experiment-ed with design ideas and concepts.

Catherine combines traditional tools and bench skills with modern techniques such as the use of photosensitive film to create well-crafted, unique and highly wearable gold and silver jewellery. She is greatly influenced by the graphic arts and her collection of wood engravings and etchings, all of which inform her jewellery designs.

Catherine loves to design brooches, as this gives her an opportunity to make something that is not only visually pleasing, but also tells a story about the environment which inspires her work.

Alexandra Twin

www.alexandratwin.co.uk   Petersfield

Wild yet constrained

Inspired by the glorious countryside, Alex is very much a country girl who loves the toughness and beauty of the wild plants that spring up everywhere unwanted and struggling for survival. These plants break the rules just a little bit and that appeals to her. This can also be seen in her work – the unruliness of the wild constrained within frames. As a child she loved long country walks with her parents, splashing through mud and climbing trees, but most importantly watching her dad's enthusiasm for carpentry became a fundamental influence on her work.

Since graduating from the University of Creative Arts, she has been building her own workshop. She feels at home sitting on the jewellery bench and loves using all the hand tools to create something from scratch.

Alex strongly believes in fairtrade practice and chooses to work with recycled silver. The idea of melting down someone's unwanted jewellery and recycling it into something new for someone else to love has tremendous appeal for her.

"I am always happiest when I am sitting on my bench trying to figure out how to make something new, so if I could do that and pay the bills what more could I ask for?"
Alexandra Twin

others

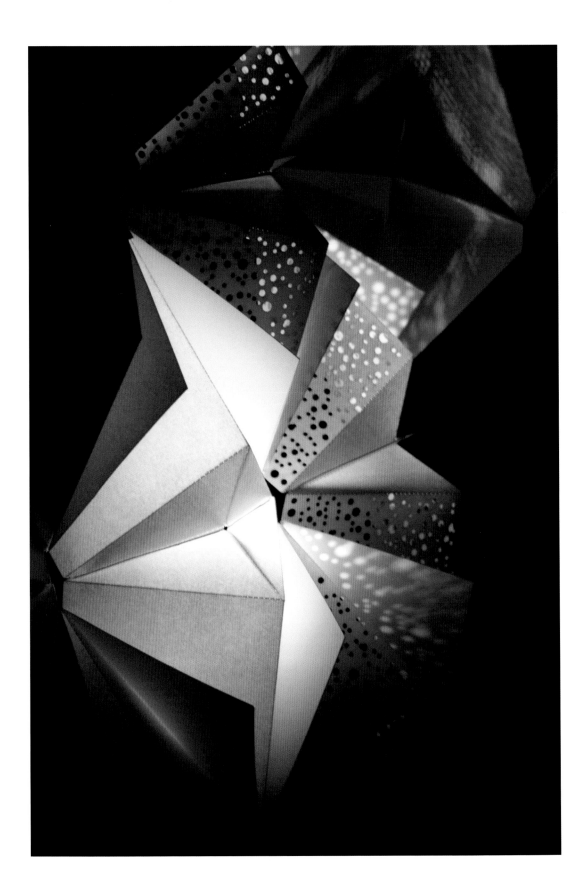

"The application of well-honed craft skills and techniques coupled with a high degree of creativity to produce the end product is the key to achieve a true combination of craft and fine art" Sharyn Dunn

Rachel Carter

www.rachelcarter.co.uk   Derbyshire

Fluid shapes of nature

Rachel grew up in a DIY environment and fondly remembers watching Blue Peter and remaking everything she saw on the show. There was also a secondhand sewing machine her mother bought her from the market which she still uses to make her children's fancy dress outfits.

She always enjoyed wood and metal work in her school, but could not pursue it further because girls weren't allowed to in her school, so she opted for hospitality instead. Some years later, however, she studied 3D Sustainable Design and Practice at the University of Derby and then set up her studio.

Rachel takes inspiration from the plants in her own garden plus trips to botanical gardens and the English countryside. She creates beautiful, fluid outdoor sculptures with willow and mild steel, which are inspired from nature. Willow rods are entwined and woven onto a welded mild steel frame to create a structural skeleton for the sculpture. Using traditional methods of metal work and weaving to marry these two materials together, she creates endless possibilities for style, shape and use. The metal frame slowly changes colour, weathered by the elements to blend seamlessly with the woven willow, which is preserved in the traditional manner, using boiled linseed oil.

Jon Cooper

www.woddenpots.co.uk   York

Modern approach to traditional wood

Jon always liked making things with wood, but he was never pleased with the amateur items made. However on a trip to the US, he was so inspired by beautiful wood-turning products that he decided to pursue it further. So, after 32 years of working in IT, he seized the opportunity for redundancy in 2010 and set himself the task of learning the challenging craft of wood turning.

His love for wood and some training in wood turning have enhanced his skills and his designs have progressed from simple open bowls to more technical and challenging designs, where he experiments with finishes and contrasting woods. Taking a contemporary approach, his designs are led to a large extent by the material and are adapted along the process.

His designs are primarily decorative, focussing on design and finishes. Regardless of the time taken, he brings the same precision and attention to detail to the inside of the bowl as he does to the outer surface, making it a beautifully finished quality product.

Often discussing his challenges and problems with his dog while working, Jon's aim is to create large art pieces and explore more textures and colours in his work.

Darkest Star

www.darkeststar.co.uk   London

'The Study of an Orchid'

Andy D'Cruze and Sam Cook combine conceptual art with functional products in their design house called *Darkest Star*. Each project is an inspirational journey of creativity taking form in a variety of artistic media such as fine art, photography, film, fashion, accessories, interiors and sculpture.

Before *Darkest Star* was formed, Sam, who studied fashion at Central Saint Martins, had been making clothes and accessories since she was nine. Her career has taken her through design studios and couture houses. Andy, who is a photographic retoucher, had worked on high profile campaigns alongside celebrated photographers.

'The Study of an Orchid' is an ongoing project where *Darkest Star* explores different avenues that always tie into the orchid theme. Their 'Pleasure Garden' project is inspired from the furor that surrounded the arrival of the first orchid in England in 1818, when anything exotic ignited excitement and titillation, and the traditional garden became a place of entertainment amongst the high society. With this project they have produced a short film, sculptures and a collection of clothing and accessories.

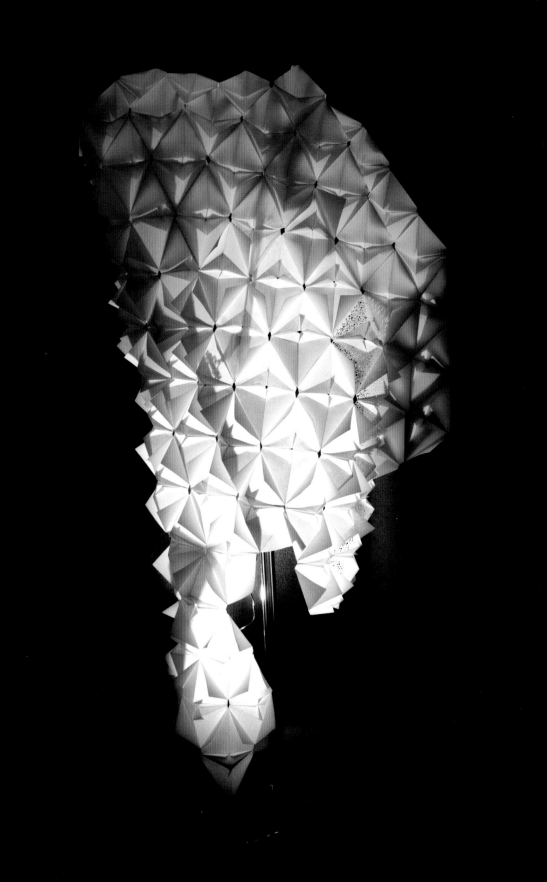

Sharyn Dunn

www.sharyndunn.com   Leicester

Interacting with light and shadow

Design has always been an integral part of Sharyn's life, whether as a teenager learning fashion and running a successful knitwear company or through her interest in interiors and producing hand-embroidered wall panels influenced by Feng Shui. All these creative influences have resulted from her degree in design crafts at De Montfort University, where she had the opportunity to expand her knowledge and skills in ceramics, glass, silversmithing, and also in textiles, paper and

metals – her current work.

In her current work she explores the interaction of light within complex geometric forms. Using a variety of materials, predominantly papers, simulated parchments, tyvek and metal, she folds and manipulates them to create geometric and organic structures that develop their own unique light and shadow effects. The designs are pierced into the structures either by hand or laser cutting and with the addition of creative lighting, the resulting sculptures provide the observer with a unique, dynamic and thought-provoking experience.

Her sculptures are generally wall-mounted or free-standing, but can also be suspended depending on the desired effect.

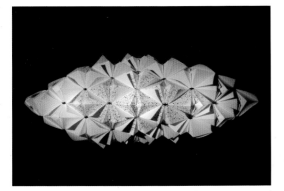

Morgan Howell

www.supersizeart.com   St. Albans

Supersize art

As a boy Morgan was captivated by his father's watercolour paintings. Inspired, he left school at 16 to study graphic design at art school. In 2005 he was made a Fellow of the Royal Society of Arts and he started *Super-SizeArt* in 2009 in addition to *The Teds Agency*, his long established advertising agency business.

The Teds work with brands such as Pioneer, Fujifilm, Harman and Filippo Berio Olive Oil, winning the U-Talk award for their memorable operatic TV commercial. Morgan's creative talent always lends the brands consummate style.

Morgan's concept of painting large facsimiles of old records and annuals led to the creation of super-sized paintings of many hand-me-down classic singles of his childhood. The artworks are large scale versions of classic 45's – mostly from the 1960's and 1970's. He paints the record covers on canvas and then re-creates all the crinkles and torn edges associated with the sleeve of an old 7 inch single along with the graphics of the original label to create a giant version of the original.

He is interested in the root of things, rediscovering and celebrating his childhood passions. But most of all he loves to be the first to think and act as new ideas excite him and keep him motivated.

His work has been sold worldwide and can be seen in galleries in St.Albans, London, Cambridge and the Netherlands.

Sarah Wollerton

www.lizzytish.co.uk   Norfolk

The plastic and metal specialist

As a child Sarah spent hours in the garden watching butterflies and was transfixed by their beautiful colours and forms. Her grandfather, an accomplished woodcarver and maker, had a huge collection of butterflies from around the world, which were displayed in fine wooden drawers like trays of jewels.

From an early age, Sarah started using tools and making things for herself and others. She studied in Brighton and specialised in plastics and metals. After the course, she took up a job at the college and was renowned for her knowledge of plastics and her mould-making skills. During that time she carried out a number of commissions including work for British Airways, the London Eye and created large scale 'body adornment' for some of the city's iconic buildings as part of Brighton's bid for the City of Culture.

Sarah is greatly inspired by processes and materials and likes to push the limits. Her best results often come from happy accidents or experimental trial and error. She is a stickler for precision and obsessed with fine detailing.

She now dedicates all her time to her brand *Lizzytish* and converts all her ideas into beautiful pieces.

Acknowledgements

First of all I would like to thank Lee Ripley, Vivays Publishing and her friendly team for their help and valuable advice on this book.

I would also like to express my gratitude to all the participating designer-makers who have made this project possible not only by providing their work and the stories they shared, but also for their interest and support for Handmade in Britain.

I sincerely thank Matthew Booth for his hard work in producing the original photographs used in the book, and for his patience in dealing with the Royal Mail and for working closely with the designers. I am also grateful to the other photographers whose work has made an important contribution to this book.

Last but not least, I am especially grateful to Tiziana Lardieri for her contribution to and enthusiasm for this project.

Photo Credits

t = top, b = bottom, c = center, l = left, tl = top left, tr = top right, bl = bottom left, br = bottom right

Front Cover © **Shannon Tofts**

© **Matthew Booth**: p.16 t, p.17, p. 18 - 19, p. 20, p. 22 - 23, p. 24 - 25, p. 26, p. 28 - 29, p. 30 t, p. 31, p. 34 bl, p. 35, p. 36, p. 38 - 39, p. 43, p. 46 - 47, p. 48, p. 52 - 53, p. 56 - 57, p. 58 - 59, p. 62, p. 64 - 65, p. 69, p. 70 - 71, p. 79, p. 80, p. 81 bl, p. 82 - 83, p. 84 - 85, p. 86 bl, p. 87, p. 90, p. 92 - 93, p. 96 tr, p. 97, p. 100 - 101, p. 106, p. 108 - 109, p. 110, p.112 - 113, p. 114 - 115, p. 116 - 117, p. 120 - 121, p. 122, p.123 bl, p. 125, p. 126, p. 128 - 129, p. 130 - 131, p. 132 - 133, p. 134 - 135, p. 136 - 137, p. 140 - 141, p. 148, p. 152, p. 153 tr, p. 154 - 155, p. 156 - 157, p. 158 tl, p. 161, p. 164, p. 165 tr, p. 170 - 171, p. 172, p. 174 - 175, p. 176 - 177, p.179, p. 180, p. 183, p. 185, p. 186, p. 188 - 189, p. 191, p. 192, p. 197, p. 200 - 201, p. 202, p. 203 tl, p. 205, p. 214 bl.

© Greenhalf Photography p. 2, p. 49, © Shan Annabelle Valla, © Sussie Ahlburg p. 6, p. 12, p. 27 c, b, p. 55, p. 181, © Richard Barnes p. 15, p. 40, © Cath Ball p.16 b, © Nicola Crocker p. 21 © Paul Persky p. 27 t, © Maria De Haan p. 30 bl, Dameon Lynn p. 18 - 19, © Paul Persky p. 23 t, © Stephen Brayne p. 32 p. 33 bl, © Cliff Van Coevorden p. 33 tr, © Zoe Hillyard p. 34 tr, © Kiff Photography p. 40 - 41, © Daniel Reynolds p. 44 - 45, © Stephen Brayne p. 51, © Jenefer Han p. 66, p. 67 tr, © Edwin Baker p. 67 bl, © David Burges p. 68, © Naomi Singer p. 72 - 73, © David Oates p. 76, © Chris Edwards p. 78, © Philip Hearsey p. 81 tr, © Tony North p. 86 br, © Tristan Harris p. 94 - 95, © Adrian McCurdy p. 96 bl, © Nina Duncan Photography p. 98 - 98, © Melanie Rye p. 102 - 103, © Rachael Jackson p.111, © Kirstin Prisk p.118 - 119, © Tim Speller p. 123 tr, © Michael Wicks p. 124, © Kate Hasted p. 127, © Marcus Holdsworth p. 138 - 139, © Alick Cotterill p. 142, © FXP Photography p. 144 - 145, p. 190, © Ruth Emily Davey p. 150 - 151, © Adam Flynn p. 153 bl, © Yu-Ping Lin p. 159, © Yuka Maeda p. 160, © Alistair Clark p. 162 - 163, © Natasha Wodzynki p. 165 bl, © Sue Gregor p. 178, © Zoe Harding p. 182, © Joël Degen p.184, p. 187 © Chris Poupazis p. 193, © Caroline Reynolds p. 194 - 195, © Simon Chapman p. 196, © Electronic Market Squares p.197 tr, © Sarah Straussberg p. 198 - 199, © Catherine Thomas p. 203, © Alexandra Twin p. 204 bl, © Al Bryden p. 208, p. 216 - 217, © Colin Bramley Photography p. 211, © Jon Cooper p. 212 - 213, © Darkest Star p. 214 tr, p. 215, © Phil Surbey p. 218 - 219, © Shot by Lucy p. 220 - 221.